FIFTY PLACES TO CAMP

BEFORE YOU DIE

FIFTY PLACES TO

CAMP

BEFORE YOU DIE

**Camping Experts Share
the World's Greatest Destinations**

Chris Santella

FOREWORD BY MIKE HARRELSON

STEWART, TABORI & CHANG

NEW YORK

This book is for my girls, Cassidy, Annabel, and Deidre,
and the many fun nights we have spent in our humongous L.L.Bean tent.

Contents

ACKNOWLEDGMENTS

This book would not have been possible without the generous assistance of the outdoor enthusiasts who shared their time and experience to help bring these fifty great camping venues to life. To these men and women, I offer the most heartfelt thanks. I also wish to acknowledge the fine efforts of my agent, Stephanie Kip Rostan, my editors Samantha Weiner and Michael Clark, assistant editor Zachary Knoll, designer Anna Christian, and copyeditor David Blatty, who helped bring the book into being. Finally, I want to extend a special thanks to my wife, Deidre, and my daughters, Cassidy and Annabel, with whom I've enjoyed many fine camping adventures (even though they tend to bring a few more accoutrements than I might pack) . . . and to my parents, Tina and Andy Santella, who have not pitched a tent for at least sixty years but have always encouraged me to pursue my passions.

OPPOSITE:

Far removed from any human settlements, the Owyhee Canyonlands in southeastern Oregon make a fine spot for stargazing . . . and enjoying a campfire.

FOREWORD

A mentor once told me, "Measure the *quality* of each year by the number of nights you camp out." Understand this sage campfire wisdom, and you will know there's something transcendent about leaving life's walls and ceilings behind to become immersed in nature; be it to defrag the mental hard drive by staring at the stars, or to calm oneself by the flow of a wild river, our senses simply become more in tune when we take a break from everyday civilization. In our topsy-turvy world, camping is a surefire way to regain your center.

Whether on a juniper-scented red rock mesa, in a bison-speckled national park, by an alpine mirror lake or a wave-salted shoreline, superlative camp spots come in a variety of flavors. There are so many attributes that distinguish a serviceable campsite from a brilliant bivouac. And sometimes, if you're willing to explore, you'll find them in the least expected places.

While some seek peace and tranquility, others look for a basecamp to adventure. Whether your camp implements of choice are a folding chair and good book, or perhaps a fishing rod, mountain bike, or canoe; whether a single, couple, or family reunion . . . there's a prime camp spot out there, waiting just for you.

This book is titled *Fifty Places to Camp Before You Die*, and let me remind you: None of us know when we're heading off for the dirt nap. Therefore, regardless of your age or the vigor of your vital signs, I suggest you get busy. Use this book as a guide and/or a "must do" tick list. And, if you're really on your game, you'll soon have fifty more of your own self-vetted recommendations to suggest to Chris for the next edition of this book.

So, how many nights will *you* camp this coming year?

—Mike Harrelson, Free Range Journalist

INTRODUCTION

At no time in history have human beings been so far removed from the natural world. In America alone, nearly 81 percent of the population now lives in an urban area. It's no wonder that many of us suffer from what writer Richard Louv termed "nature deficit disorder" in his 2005 book, *Last Child in the Woods*.

Camping provides an opportunity to take on nature deficit disorder directly. To retreat from the trials of day-to-day life to a simpler existence. To refuel and reinvigorate amongst the wonders of nature, be it at the seashore, in the mountains, or in the desert.

I wrote *Fifty Places to Camp Before You Die* for those who appreciate the chance to experience the great outdoors with family, with friends . . . or all by themselves.

"What makes a destination a place you have to camp before you die?" you might ask. The chance to take in incredible scenery and immerse oneself in the natural world? To enjoy time away from fellow humans or time with wild creatures? An opportunity to pursue a favorite outdoor pastime with the flexibility (and economy) that a tent provides? Or perhaps enjoy the special camaraderie that occurs around a blazing fire, where the biggest concern is not overcooking your marshmallow? The answer would be yes to all of the above, and an abundance of other criteria. One thing I knew when I began this project: I was not the person to assemble this list. So I followed a recipe that served me well in my first eleven Fifty Places books—to seek the advice of some outdoor professionals. To write *Fifty Places to Camp Before You Die*, I interviewed a host of people closely connected with the camping world and asked them to share some of their favorite experiences. These experts range from National Park Service employees (like Jackie Skaggs, Charlie Jacobi, and Kari Cobb) to leaders in the outdoor-equipment industry (like Rich Hill, Christopher Martens, and Kirk Richardson). Some spoke of venues that are near and dear to their hearts, places where they've built their professional reputations; others spoke of places they've only visited once, but which made a profound impression. People appreciate camping for many different reasons, and this range of attractions is evidenced here. (To give a sense of the breadth of the interviewees' backgrounds, a bio of each individual is included after each essay.)

Camping means different things to different people. For some, it may mean an isolated, no-frills site where you have to bring in your own water, and you're more likely to

encounter a bighorn sheep than a blasting boombox; for others, it may mean a camp-ground with full amenities, an ongoing ranger program, and a lodge nearby for those nights when you just don't feel like cooking . . . and perhaps even the option of a cabin for those who don't feel quite like tenting. *Fifty Places to Camp Before You Die* attempts to capture the spectrum of camping experiences. While the book collects fifty great venues, it by no means attempts to rank the places discussed or the quality of the experiences they afford. Such ranking is, of course, largely subjective.

In the hope that a few readers might embark on their own camping adventures, I have provided brief "If You Go" information at the end of each chapter, including an overview of the amenities available and recommended activities for campers. The "If You Go" information is by no means a comprehensive list, but should give would-be travelers a starting point for planning their trip. (Most national and state parks require an entry fee, and licenses may be required for fishing and other activities. Please visit the websites for the region you're planning to visit for the most current pricing/regulations.)

One needn't travel to the ends of the earth to find a rewarding camping experience. A quick overnight jaunt to a state or county park outside the city limits can often be enough to recharge your batteries for the week ahead. Yet a trip to a dream venue can create memories for a lifetime. It's my hope that this little book will inspire you to embark on some new camping adventures of your own.

OPPOSITE:
Longitude 131°,
in the shadow of
Kata Tjuta (Ayers
Rock), offers one
of the world's most
unique glamping
experiences.

NEXT PAGE:
Mist lifts from an
Adirondack lake
on a crisp fall
morning.

The Destinations

POINT AMARGURA CABIN

RECOMMENDED BY **Ellen Hannan**

There are many fine ways to experience the wonderful wildlife and scenic grandeur of Southeast Alaska. More than a dozen cruise-ship lines offer tours of the Inside Passage and (in the case of smaller ships) its thousands of miles of nooks and crannies. A number of lodges host anglers and wildlife watchers, providing a mix of sport-fishing outings and flightseeing excursions. Still others choose to explore segments of the five-hundred-mile passage by kayak, paddling their way from fjord to fjord and camping along the way.

One of the most economical—yet still adventurous—ways to experience the dramatic beauty of Southeast Alaska and the Tongass National Forest is to rent one of the forest cabins operated by the U.S. Forest Service.

"I grew up in Anchorage and have lived on Prince of Wales Island for thirty years," Ellen Hannan began. "During the summer, I work as a commercial fisherwoman in the waters around the region, but I also love to recreate here. The Forest Service cabin at Point Amargura is one of my favorite spots to make a base camp. It has great access to lots of areas to fish and explore. Having the cabin is great, given the kind of weather we have in Southeast. There used to be an old A-frame cabin on the site, but now it's been upgraded. It's larger and more weathertight. You can go out there in May or October—often the only time I have off in the warmer months because of our fishing schedule—throw up a tarp outside for a cooking area, and be very comfortable."

The Tongass National Forest occupies 16.8 million acres, stretching 500 miles from the Dixon Entrance at the border with British Columbia north to the town of Yakutat. Often referred to as the panhandle of Alaska, this region—larger than Massachusetts, New Hampshire, and Vermont combined—includes rugged mountains, ice fields, and glaciers, and more than 11,000 miles of coastline, spread over more than 1,000 islands.

OPPOSITE:
Campers at
Point Amargura
will want to
keep their eyes
and ears open
for humpback
whales, which
will approach
quite close to
the cabin.

(When many think of Alaska, this is the terrain they're envisioning.) Given the breadth of the landscape and the fact that there are only 70,000 residents in Southeast Alaska—and very few roads—it's not hard to find a bit of solitude in the wilderness. Such forays are facilitated by the presence of more than 180 cabins scattered around the region. A number of cabins and three-sided shelters were constructed by the Civilian Conservation Corps (CCC) in the 1930s, both to provide employment for out-of-work Alaskans and to create accessible, economical recreational outlets; the 1960s saw another uptick of cabin construction. The Southeast Alaska climate is not easy on structures; annual rainfall in sections of this temperate rain forest can exceed 120 inches! But the Forest Service is diligent about maintaining—and when necessary, rebuilding—the cabins for visitor use.

Point Amargura Cabin rests on the southern tip of San Fernando Island, which is eight miles west of Craig, the largest settlement on nearby Prince of Wales Island. Ample by Forest Service cabin standards, the 255-square-foot cabin boasts a loft area and can sleep up to six visitors. It comes equipped with a wood stove for heating purposes, an axe and wedges for splitting firewood, and an outhouse a convenient distance away. If you're lucky, previous visitors may have laid in some firewood for your use. "We have a group of friends who usually head out to Amargura around Memorial Day each year," Ellen continued. "Part of the trip is fun, but we also do some work to neaten things up around the cabin. We clear away debris to improve access to the beach, and we cut a bunch of firewood. The unofficial rule is that you leave more firewood than you use." While you may find wood at Point Amargura (or the other Forest Service cabin of your choice), you'll have to bring everything else—drinking water, sleeping bags and pads, cooking stove, lantern, kitchen supplies, toilet paper, etc.

Perhaps the greatest feature of the Point Amargura Cabin is its proximity to the water that supports so much life here. The Ursua Channel ebbs and floods outside the cabin, occasionally bringing seaborne visitors almost to your door. "There have been several occasions where friends and I have been sitting around the fire outside, and it's very quiet," Ellen recalled. "It could be in the evening or the morning. Suddenly we'll hear the sound of a whale blowing water, very close, and soon there's a humpback whale right at the point, by the kelp beds. They can really sneak up." Reduced to a population of fewer than 1,500 whales by the mid-60s, the North Pacific population of humpbacks has rebounded to more than 20,000 individuals.

Humpbacks may be the most dramatic surface performers among Alaska's cetaceans, breaching, tail and pectoral fin slapping, and spy hopping (where the whale keeps its head out of the water to observe goings-on), and pods are present year-round. "We've also had some nice killer-whale experiences around Point Amargura," Ellen added. "We were in the boat in a very shallow area among some kelp beds. The water wasn't much more than six feet deep. A pod of forty or fifty orcas came through. It took a while for them to pass; they were strung out quite a distance."

Some of the sea life you'll encounter around Point Amargura will most likely be at the end of a fishing line. If you've traveled to San Fernando Island with a boat or kayak, you'll be near fertile fishing grounds. Halibut, lingcod, and four salmon species—pink, chum, silver, and Chinook (king)—can all be found here. Bring strong gear, as kings can grow to more than fifty pounds and halibut to more than two hundred!

The tides of Southeast Alaska are extreme and can vary more than twenty feet. During high tide (the only time you can bring a floatplane or boat to shore at Point Amargura), plan on being in your boat or cabin . . . the cabin backs up against a cliff, and there are no maintained trails through the thick forest of Sitka spruce and western hemlock. But when the tide is out, beachcombing opportunities abound. "When enrollment in the Craig schools (on Prince of Wales Island) was smaller, I'd take our high school students out to Point Amargura," Ellen shared. "We'd go on the big minus tides and do beach exploration. It was the culmination of our science studies."

ELLEN HANNAN is a former schoolteacher, commercial fisherwoman, and technology educator based in Craig, Alaska. An Alaskan since age two, she is a member of the Nanook Hall of Fame, in recognition for her outstanding achievements as a collegiate basketball player for the University of Alaska Fairbanks.

If You Go

▶ **Getting There:** Point Amargura can be reached by boat or floatplane from the town of Craig on Prince of Wales Island, or by floatplane from Ketchikan. Ketchikan is served by Alaska Airlines (800-252-7522; www.alaskaair.com); Island Air Express (888-387-8989;

https://islandairx.com) provides service from Ketchikan to Craig. A number of boat charter services are available in Craig.

► **Best Time to Visit:** Point Amargura Cabin is open year-round, though peak season is considered May through September.

► **Campgrounds:** Point Amargura Cabin is among more than 180 U.S. Forest Service cabins available in the Tongass National Forest. It comes equipped with a table, benches, a wood stove for heat, and an outside toilet; a fire extinguisher, an axe, and a broom are also provided. You'll have to bring everything else, including water. Rentals are $35 in peak season, $25 during off-season, and can be reserved through ReserveAmerica (877-444-6777; www.reserveamerica.com).

► **Activities:** Wildlife viewing, fishing, hunting, beachcombing, boating.

► **Note:** There are very few black bears and no grizzly bears on San Fernando Island.

DENALI NATIONAL PARK

RECOMMENDED BY **Kris Fister**

At 20,320 feet, Mount McKinley towers high above the Alaskan tundra. On clear days, the great massif can be spied from downtown Anchorage, some two hundred miles away. Yet it's a special thrill to gaze upon McKinley—now more recognized as *Denali*, or "the High One" in the Athabascan language—from a more immediate perspective. That's but one of the appeals of a visit to Denali National Park.

"Denali has facilities like a park in the Lower 48, but it's also a very wild place," began Kris Fister. "There's little in the way of hiking trails, but the park road cuts through the vast wilderness and provides many chances to see Alaska's iconic animals. The landscape here is a great introduction to Alaska. It's on a whole different scale."

Denali National Park and Preserve (originally Mount McKinley National Park) was dedicated in 1917; it now extends to more than six million acres in interior Alaska. Denali has the distinction of being the first park set aside specifically for the preservation of its animal life and owes its existence to the vision of a gentleman hunter named Charles Sheldon and an outdoorsman named Harry Karstens. After spending the winter of 1907 in a cabin near the Toklat River, the two hatched the idea for the park. It took ten years for their idea to find purchase, but since that time, animals within the park's boundaries have thrived. High on many visitor "must-see" lists are the "Denali Big Five"—grizzly bear, Dall's sheep, caribou, moose, and wolf. "I've had a number of days when I'll see one or more of the big five on my drive into work," Kris continued. "If you take the bus all the way to Wonder Lake and pay close attention, you have a decent chance of coming into contact with all five."

There is only one road in Denali—a distinctive feature among national parks—and the National Park Service has created a system to ensure that it's a first-class wildlife

viewing highway. "The road is ninety-two miles long and goes from the park entrance to the historic mining district of Kantishna," Kris explained. "It parallels the Alaska Range, and there are several spots along the way where you can see Mount McKinley if the skies are clear, though this is generally not the case. Private vehicles are allowed on the first fifteen miles of road to the Savage River. Beyond this point, travel is restricted to buses operated by the park concessionaire, private lodges in Kantishna, and private vehicles with administrative road permits. You might come upon animals in that first fifteen miles, especially early in the season, but your odds are far greater once you're past milepost fifteen." There are several bus options: Shuttle busses run to different destinations along the length of the road and will stop to let passengers view wildlife, snap photos of striking scenery, and disembark to hike. If you have a shuttle-bus pass, you can catch buses going east or west as far as your ticket destination. Tour buses provide a more structured experience, with narration by the driver, and set travel routes. One trip takes you seventeen miles along the road (four to five hours), another fifty-three miles (seven to eight hours), a third the entire road (eleven to twelve hours). Visitors also have the option of biking the road past Savage River, a mode of travel that's seeing increasing popularity. "Animals do walk the road, however," Kris cautioned. "If you're on a bike and a bear is on the road, you had better wait for it to pass . . . or head in the opposite direction!"

There are six road-accessible campgrounds in Denali, offering a range of experiences. "Riley Creek is the biggest," Kris continued. "It's near the entrance to the park road, just a half mile from the George Parks Highway, and has the most amenities, including easy access to the Mercantile convenience store, laundry, showers, and Wi-Fi access. On the other end of the spectrum is Wonder Lake. It's the most remote campground, located at milepost eighty-five on the park road. You need to take the shuttle bus out there. The terrain is a little different here, less forested and at a lower elevation than most of the campgrounds in the park. Late in the summer, there may be an abundant crop of blueberries to enjoy. There are just twenty-nine sites here, but there are flush toilets and lovely shelters that you can cook under and where you can store uneaten food (and toothpaste and other scented items). Wonder Lake is the closest campground to McKinley, just twenty-five miles away. It's often cloudy, but when the skies do clear, the view is incredible. Sometimes you'll get up in the middle of the night to go to the bathroom and the mountain is right there in all its glory; in the summer, it's light most of the time. (Savage River is the only other

OPPOSITE:
Denali—"the
High One"—
is the tallest
mountain in
North America
at 20,310 feet.

campground you can see McKinley from.) There are lots of little ponds and lakes in addition to Wonder Lake itself, and the mosquitoes out there can be quite abundant. I try to avoid going out there in July. I've watched visitors travel all the way out there on the bus with their camping gear, step outside, and within minutes, get back on the bus. But in late August, the mosquitoes are done and the fall colors are brilliant. The Teklanika River Campground is roughly thirty miles into the park; you can drive there, but you have to stay a minimum of three nights to minimize road traffic. The Teklanika is a beautiful braided river, and it's not uncommon to come upon wolves and bear while hiking along it."

Though Denali may not offer as many miles of trails as other parks, it does offer some interesting hiking opportunities. "One of our most popular ranger programs is the day-long Discovery Hike," Kris explained. "The group size is limited to eleven people, and venues are ever changing. Descriptions of the hike and what you should bring clothing-wise are available when you sign up. Then you get on the shuttle bus and ride to the appointed meeting place and meet the ranger leading the hike. When you're hiking out on the tundra, there's nothing between you and the wildlife and weather. You really feel that you're part of the landscape. When I'm out there, I'm constantly scanning for bears—you never forget that. You get a brief respite when you reach a higher spot and can see around you. There's the sense that nothing will sneak up on you for a while.

"Another unique ranger program at Denali is the sled-dog demonstration. We have a working sled-dog kennel; the dogs provide transportation into wilderness areas in the park where snow machines are not allowed. During the demonstration, visitors can meet some of the huskies that work at the park and see a ranger mush a team on a short loop [albeit without snow] and learn how we use the dogs to help protect the park."

KRIS FISTER worked at outdoor education centers and state parks in Ohio, Vermont, and New Hampshire before moving to California in 1980 to take an instructor position at Yosemite Institute, an outdoor education program based in Yosemite National Park. In 1982 she accepted her first position with the National Park Service, as a seasonal park ranger in Yosemite's Mariposa Grove of Giant Sequoias. Within a few years, Kris was working year-round for the NPS. She accepted a permanent job in Yosemite's Public Information Office in 1990 and was serving as public information officer when she left in January 1996 to take her first position supervising the West District interpretive operation at Denali National Park and Preserve in Alaska. Working and living in the heart of the park was an extraordinary experience. She returned to California in the summer of 1998 to become Sequoia/Kings Canyon's first public affairs officer and enjoyed spending time again in the big trees, hiking and skiing in the southern Sierra Nevada. But Kris missed Alaska and returned to Denali in 2003 as its public affairs officer, a position she still holds.

If You Go

▶ **Getting There:** Visitors can fly into Anchorage or Fairbanks. Anchorage (240 miles south) is served by many carriers; Fairbanks (120 miles north) is served by Alaska Airlines (800-252-7522; www.alaskaair.com) and Delta (800-221-1212; www.delta.com).

▶ **Best Time to Visit:** Peak season is early June through mid-September; shuttle buses are running at this time. Riley Creek Campground is open year-round, though only heartier campers will enjoy the shoulder seasons or winter. See details at www.nps.gov/dena.

▶ **Campgrounds:** There are six campgrounds within Denali, with options for both tents and RVs. Fees range from $9 to $28; reservations can be made via www.reservedenali. com or by calling 800-622-7275.

▶ **Activities:** Wildlife viewing, hiking, and biking. Ranger-led activities include hikes and sled-dog demonstrations.

JASPER NATIONAL PARK

RECOMMENDED BY **Nancy Smith**

The Icefields Parkway, which stretches 130 miles from Lake Louise in Banff National Park to the town of Jasper in Jasper National Park, is among the world's most beautiful roads. Skirting the Continental Divide, it courses past some 100 glaciers, countless dizzying mountains, pristine glacial lakes, and a combined wilderness of 6,899 square miles that's home to countless totemic animals of the Canadian Rockies, including elk, caribou, bighorn sheep, black and grizzly bears, and wolves. Near the parkway's midpoint—just a few miles inside the border of Jasper National Park—sits the Columbia Icefield . . . one of Nancy Smith's favorite places to pitch a tent.

"I love the Columbia Icefield for its location," she began. "It's really central between Banff and Jasper, and you have great accessibility to a number of wonderful hikes for people of all levels. And when you wake up and go to bed, you can look out at that tremendous glacier. It's always different, depending on the light."

The largest of Canada's Rocky Mountain Parks, Jasper encompasses 4,335 square miles of wilderness terrain, spread along the eastern slopes of the Canadian Rockies. Jasper holds a similar space for Canadians as Yellowstone does for Americans. It's a place where automobile passengers have a great chance to encounter wildlife along the road as well as in the backcountry, and it offers some startling natural phenomena, like Athabasca Falls and the Columbia Icefield. Of course, there are also hundreds of miles of hiking and biking trails, opportunities to ride horses or to fish, and a charming resort town in the middle of the park, fittingly named Jasper.

Jasper's eleven campgrounds offer a range of amenities. Whistlers and Wapiti, near the town of Jasper, can accommodate RVs up to thirty-nine feet and offer hookups; Whistlers also features new "cottage tents," a great option for new campers to ease their

OPPOSITE:
Jaw-dropping
Canadian Rocky
views await you
at every turn
in Jasper
National Park.

way into the outdoor lifestyle. All campgrounds—including primitive sites—offer fire-wood, bear-proof lockers, and log cookhouses for prepping meals during inclement weather. There are two campgrounds near the Columbia Icefield—Columbia Icefield (tent camping only) and Wilcox Creek (mixed use). More than just a great location, these venues offer walking access to one of Jasper's most unique attractions.

The Columbia Icefield covers more than 125 square miles, reaching depths of nearly 1,200 feet in places. It's the remnant of an ice mass that's believed to have covered much of western Canada's mountains; its location (and size) is explained in part by its proximity to a number of Jasper's highest peaks, which serve to trap moisture carried across British Columbia from the Pacific. The Columbia Icefield feeds eight major glaciers, including Athabasca; since Athabasca borders the parkway, it is the most visited glacier in North America. (An interesting hydrological fact: the Columbia Icefield sends water to three different oceans—the Atlantic [via the North Saskatchewan River and Hudson Bay], the Arctic [via the Athabasca], and the Pacific [via the Columbia River]). "There are lots of ways that visitors can experience the icefield," Nancy continued. "You can hike up a section of Athabasca Glacier right from the parking lot. If you have extra time, you can take a snowcoach (a vehicle specially designed for snow travel) up farther onto the ice. Some tour companies will even lead you on an ice walk. There's a brand-new attraction at the icefield called the Skywalk. It's a glass-bottomed structure that juts out over the ice so people with limited mobility can experience the glacier."

For Nancy, most camping trips to Jasper involve a fair bit of time on the trail. She shared a few of her favorite hikes from the six-hundred-plus miles of trails that Jasper has to offer. "From near Columbia Icefield, you have great hikes available for people of all abilities. If you have children, I would suggest Parker Ridge. It's beautifully groomed, the grade is moderate, and it's only about three miles. After you reach the ridge, there's a sensational view of the Saskatchewan Glacier, Castleguard Mountain, and Mount Saskatchewan. You'll see people of all ages and walks of life on this trail. Though it's not long, it gives you a great sense of accomplishment. If you're looking for a bit more of a challenge, I like Wilcox Pass. One thing I enjoy about hiking is the transition between different ecozones. With this hike, you begin in the forest with the scent of pines. As you gain elevation, you get above tree line and the trail opens up to outstanding views of meadows and the icefield. There are abundant wildflowers, and sometimes you'll see bighorn sheep. If you're looking for a more serious backcountry hike, there's the Skyline

Trail. It's a three-day trip, ideally; you follow a ridge from summit to summit, with constant stunning views of the Rockies."

Summer days linger long in Jasper National Park. The sun rises near five a.m. and doesn't set until ten p.m. "You don't want the day to end," Nancy confided. "But the good news is it doesn't. You hear people talk about Montana for its big sky, and we've got the same thing here. Our night sky can be spectacular. In Jasper, you're so far from any urban center that you get a truly dark sky, and you'll see stars like you've never seen them. In 2011, Jasper was designated a Dark Sky Preserve, the largest in the world." To maintain this designation, Jasper vows to support responsible lighting within the park and encourage public awareness; to this end, Jasper celebrates the Dark Sky Festival each October.

Athabasca Glacier, incidentally, is one of the premier road-accessible stargazing sites in the park.

Note: Thanks to a warming climate, the Athabasca Glacier has lost half its volume in the last 125 years. See it soon!

NANCY SMITH is a native Albertan and has worked at Travel Alberta for thirteen years. She is a passionate advocate for the authentic experiences and diversity of breathtaking landscapes the province offers visitors from around the world.

If You Go

▶ **Getting There:** Calgary is served by many major carriers, including Air Canada (888-247-2262; www.aircanada.com); Alaska Airlines (800-252-7522; www.alaskaair.com); and Delta (800-221-1212; www.delta.com).

▶ **Best Time to Visit:** There are campgrounds open in Jasper from early May through mid-October. Most trails are clear of snow by early June.

▶ **Campgrounds:** There are eleven campgrounds in Jasper. Columbia Icefield Campground is classified as primitive, with pit toilets and potable water. Sites in Jasper without hookups range from $15.70 to $27.40 (CAD).

▶ **Activities:** Hiking, wildlife viewing, boating, river rafting, horseback riding, rock climbing, and fishing.

GRAND CANYON NATIONAL PARK

RECOMMENDED BY **Kirby-Lynn Shedlowski**

Neither the deepest nor the widest gorge in the world, the Grand Canyon is nonetheless recognized as one of the planet's most awe-inspiring erosion events—a 277-mile-long chasm that yawns from 4 to 18 miles and reaches depths of more than a mile, and a seemingly endless series of gentle slopes and abrupt cliffs. "The majority of our visitors have their breath taken away when they see the expanse of Grand Canyon for the first time," Kirby-Lynn Shedlowski began. "The dramatic colors, the immense size, the natural quiet (depending on where they see the canyon for the first time), and a sense of how large the world is. I think people leave impressed with the human history of the Grand Canyon, starting with the Native Americans who lived here, working forward in history. It's impressive to view this place and begin to understand the adaptations that people have made in order to live here."

Suffice it to say, the Grand Canyon has been around a very long time. Some rocks at the bottom of the canyon date back more than 1.84 billion years, to a time before there were continents. Archaeologists have uncovered artifacts that suggest humans have used the canyon for 12,000 years. Though early Spanish explorers recorded visiting the Grand Canyon area as early as the 1540s, it was not until after Major John Wesley Powell's epic 1869 expedition that the American public came to recognize this treasure of the southwest. Powell—who'd lost his right arm during the Civil War at the Battle of Shiloh—traveled some 900 miles with a small, makeshift crew, launching on the Green River in Wyoming and leaving the canyon about three months later, physically and mentally spent. The 1,904-square-mile area was championed as a potential national park by Theodore Roosevelt, though it did not achieve park status until Woodrow Wilson wrote it into law in 1919.

OPPOSITE:
Hikers look out
over the canyon
from Cedar
Ridge, on
the South
Kaibab Trail.

31

BUFFALO NATIONAL RIVER

RECOMMENDED BY **Jill Rohrbach**

Many of us have a place that brings us a special sense of inner peace, a sanctum from the stresses of everyday life. For Jill Rohrbach, that place is the Buffalo National River.

"When I drive into the Buffalo National River Valley and get that first glimpse of the river, I take a deeper-than-normal breath, exhale, and relax," Jill began. "A sense of peacefulness and connectedness sweeps over me. It's not just the visual splendor of the place. There's something about it that you feel inside. It grabs you all the way to your bones. I never get tired of visiting the Buffalo; it always gives you a different experience. I used to go backpacking there with my husband before we had children; now we take the kids and camp in campgrounds. Either way, it's a place that lets you unplug."

The Buffalo River flows some 150 miles across northern Arkansas, beginning in the Ozark Mountains and flowing in an eastward direction until it joins the White River. The last 132 miles and their surroundings are managed by the National Park Service as one of only five rivers with the "national river" designation; the Buffalo was in fact the first river to be so recognized. The act of Congress sanctioning the national river concept came about as a response to numerous attempts to dam the river to stem flooding in the surrounding valleys. Opposition to damming the Buffalo gained momentum through the 1950s and garnered national attention after U.S. Supreme Court Justice William O. Douglas canoed the river in 1962 and declared, "You cannot let this river die. The Buffalo River is a national treasure worth fighting to the death to preserve."

Today, the undammed river continues to be a principal attraction for outdoors enthusiasts visiting the area. Twenty-two put-ins (access points) spread through three districts allow canoeists, kayakers, and inner-tubers to float a morning, an afternoon, all day, or several days. Canoes are available for rent from several concessionaires along the Buffalo.

"People will float the entire river," Jill continued. "You can be dropped off at the top and picked up at the bottom eight or nine days later." Wilderness-style camping is allowed at most points along the river for multiday sojourners, so long as campers adhere to a "leave-no-trace" ethos. The most popular multiday canoeing adventure is from Ponca to Pruitt, a twenty-six-mile float that takes in some of the Buffalo's most impressive scenery, including the 209-foot Hemmed-In Hollow waterfall. (To reach the falls from the river, visitors need to hike roughly three-quarters of a mile up a well-marked trail.)

Whether you're out for an afternoon or a week, paddlers will pass towering bluffs—including 550-foot-tall Big Bluff—and steep, wooded hillsides. The first fifteen miles of the river, which rest outside of the national river corridor (but are protected under the National Scenic River designation), are popular with white-water enthusiasts. Below this section, the river is more manageable for casual paddlers, especially in later spring and summer, as flows decrease. Floating the Buffalo, you might also come across herds of grazing elk along the meadows that cover the bottomlands; Rocky Mountain elk were introduced into the corridor in the early 1980s in an effort to replace the eastern elk that once called this region home. Today the elk population along the Buffalo is nearly five hundred. (If you're staying off the water during your visit, the roads through Boxley Valley provide a good opportunity to view these majestic ungulates. "During the rut, it's exciting to see the bull elk run each other off and hear them bugling," Jill added.)

Some of the attractions of the Buffalo rest beneath its surface—fishing is one of the corridor's most popular pastimes. Smallmouth bass are the primary quarry here; they respond well to both lures and flies and are scrappy fighters that are quick to take to the air in battle. As you make your way downriver, anglers will also encounter largemouth and spotted bass; catfish are present throughout the system.

There are abundant camping options through the river's 132-mile course. In addition to the abundant gravel bars that offer canoeists and kayakers a place to pitch a tent, the National Park Service provides nine developed campgrounds and several other primitive campgrounds with limited services. Nearly all the campgrounds are along the river. "Getting a site right by the water is a treat," Jill said. "Whether you're planning to fish or just skipping rocks. My favorite place to camp is Steel Creek. There are sites for tent campers and equestrians, and the campground looks out on Roark Bluff. There's a great swimming spot at a pool that forms at the foot of the bluff. Steel Creek is a good jumping off point for canoe day trips, and there are some fine hikes that begin fairly close by." A few of these hikes include

Hawksbill Crag, which takes you to Arkansas's most photographed landmark (of the same name) and Glory Hole, a waterfall that plummets through the top of a cave. Another hike that Jill and her family enjoy is the Lost Valley Trail, a roughly two-mile round-trip trail that leads into a box canyon festooned with wildflowers. "There's a cave at the end," Jill added, "and we usually take flashlights to do a little exploring."

In addition to its water attractions and natural beauty, the Buffalo National River corridor has a rich cultural history. Humans have occupied the corridor's bluffs and bottomlands for more than ten thousand years. Before European settlers arrived, the region was used by several Native American tribes, including the Osage, Cherokee, and Shawnee peoples. The Buffalo was also the site of several Civil War skirmishes. Though many older structures were destroyed during these skirmishes, a number of historic homes remain, including the James A. Villines Log House and the structures at the mining ghost town of Rush.

JILL ROHRBACH is a staff writer for the Arkansas Department of Parks and Tourism, editor of the online travel site OutdoorsyAdventures.com, and a freelance writer and photographer based in Fayetteville, Arkansas. Her work has been featured in publications such as *US Airways*, *Cloud 9*, and *Arkansas Good Roads*. She loves writing about outdoor adventures but has never turned down an assignment on spas, dining, or shopping either. Married with two young boys, Jill and her husband, Mike, own the Flying Burrito Company restaurants in northwest Arkansas and the bar Kingfish in Fayetteville.

If You Go

▶ **Getting There:** Many visitors will fly into Little Rock, which is roughly two hours from the Buffalo National River corridor.

▶ **Best Time to Visit:** Most of the campgrounds here are open from mid-March through mid-November. Early spring is best for white water and waterfalls; summer for swimming and mellower floating; fall colors are spectacular.

▶ **Campgrounds:** Camping in Buffalo National River's developed campgrounds is $12/ night; no fees are charged at primitive campgrounds or for riverside camping.

▶ **Activities:** Canoeing/kayaking, swimming, fishing, hiking, horseback riding, wildlife viewing.

OPPOSITE:
Boaters relax
along the Buffalo
River on a lazy
summer day.

BOODEREE NATIONAL PARK

RECOMMENDED BY **John Harvey**

In the Dhurga language, "Booderee" means "Bay of Plenty." For the Aboriginal people who have long called this place home, the "plenty" alluded to the abundant fish available for harvest. For modern-day campers, it speaks to the abundant offerings of the national park—brilliant white sand beaches, intact bush environments, well-provisioned camp-grounds, and opportunities to learn about the lifestyle of the people who've been here for thousands of years.

"Though it's just three hours south of Sydney [population 4.5 million], Booderee remains a very natural setting," John Harvey began. "The national park isn't quite an island, but a narrow neck of land that's almost entirely surrounded by water. On one side of the isthmus—St. Georges Basin to the west and part of Jervis Bay to the east—the water is very calm. These estuaries are important breeding areas for a variety of fish species, prawns, and other marine life. No commercial fishing is allowed here; it's fairly easy to go out and catch some fish and barbecue a fresh meal. On the ocean side there are sandstone cliffs climbing to one hundred meters [328 feet], remote beaches and some famous surfing breaks. Where Booderee sticks out into the Pacific, the East Australian Current mixes with cold water from the south. This makes it a hot spot for both marine and land biodiversity. There are thirty miles of bushwalking trails of different lengths, depending on what level of challenge you're seeking. Many begin at the campgrounds. In the center of the park there's a botanical garden with freshwater lakes that attract more than two hundred bird species. Lastly, the sites in our campgrounds are very private, with vegetation providing a nice buffer between sites. They are close to the beach and have modern facilities."

Booderee National Park rests in the Jervis Bay Territory of New South Wales, equidistant from the cities of Brisbane and Sydney. The twenty-four square miles occupied by the park

OPPOSITE:
Booderee is
celebrated
for some of
Australia's most
beautiful beaches,
including
Summercloud
Bay.

have historically belonged to the Wreck Bay Aboriginal community. It was originally recognized as Jervis Bay National Park in 1992 and administered by the Department of Environment and Heritage Protection. In 1995, the park was returned to the Wreck Bay community (which leases the land back to the government) and renamed Booderee. "The Aboriginal culture around Booderee is still strong, and the Wreck Bay community has a powerful connection with the land," John continued. "There are a number of ways for visitors to experience the culture. Some families have set up tour businesses where you can learn about the area's geologic origins and the region's flora and fauna, including medicinal use of plants. You can also attend a weaving workshop or a campfire storytelling session."

For most campers traveling to Australia, two experiences are high on the checklist—interacting with some of the continent's marsupials and visiting its pristine beaches. Booderee National Park delivers on both counts. "We have three species of both kangaroos and wallabies in the park, and they are quite plentiful," John explained. "It's not a question of 'if' you'll see them; it's guaranteed. Though they're wild animals and are not enclosed in any way, they often show up around the camping areas, especially at Green Patch, as there's nice grass there for the marsupials to graze on. There's also a variety of possums, and also echidnas, an anteater with protruding spines. [It's the only mammal other than the platypus that lays eggs.] Our birdlife is also notable and includes white-bellied sea eagles, kookaburras, and a number of honeyeaters.

"We are very proud of our beaches here at Booderee. There are ten altogether, and they've been declared amongst the whitest sand beaches in the world. The water quality on both the Jervis Bay and the ocean sides is exceptional. There are no river systems coming in, so there's little runoff, and there's a constant flush from the ocean currents. Diving and snorkeling are very popular, thanks to water clarity, and there are plenty of grass beds, soft corals, and sponge beds to explore, all populated by a great diversity of fish species. On the ocean side, there are many sea caves, due to the sandstone substrate. Some of the caves have significance for the Aboriginal people. The ocean side is also popular with surfers. One of Australia's better-known surf breaks, the Aussie Pipe—also known as Black Rock, Wreck Bay, and Summercloud Bay—is adjacent to the Wreck Bay community just outside the park borders. The Aboriginal kids are some of the most amazing surfers." (Cave Beach is a popular spot for beginners.)

An added bonus arrives in June and July and then again in September and October with the migration of the humpback whales. "The humpbacks come by en route to

Queensland, where they calve, and they often move close to land to have a rest," John added. "On the way back to Antarctica, the whales have their newborns with them, and they'll stop in our sheltered bays. They're very active on the surface, breaching and tail slapping." One of the best places to look for humpbacks is the Cape St. George lighthouse, which dates back to the early 1860s.

There are three campgrounds at Booderee, all with excellent beach access. Green Patch and Bristol Point rest on the calm inner waters of Jervis Bay. "Green Patch is probably our most popular campground," John said. "It was developed for RVs and camper trailers as well as tents. Bristol Point is nearby and is geared for tent campers. You have to walk your gear in a short way. Cave Beach is on the ocean side of the park. Guests there have to walk about three hundred yards to their campsite. The sites are close to the ocean; you have a sense that you're camping on a surfing beach." Green Patch and Bristol Point offer hot showers; Cave Beach campers will have to do with cold showers.

"During my time here at Booderee, I've had my eyes opened to the Aboriginal world view and how it connects so closely with the surrounding land," John opined. "I recall an evening at one of my favorite campsites at Bristol Point. It was a full-moon night silhouetting tall trees, and one of the Koori community members was sharing stories—people describe it as a campfire yarn. She was serving damper (Australian soda bread) with homemade lilly pilly jam (made from berries from a local plant) and talking about growing up on this land as a Koori person, surviving here before modern conveniences. It can be a life-changing experience, even for people who grew up in Australia. Some people from Sydney and Brisbane grew up thinking that the Aboriginal culture didn't survive, but in this enclave, it has."

JOHN HARVEY is visitor service manager at Booderee National Park, where he has worked since 2007. Before coming to Booderee, he was operations manager at Uluru-Kata Tjuta National Park, and served as a community development officer for the Mutitjulu community.

If You Go

▶ **Getting There:** Booderee National Park is three hours from Sydney, which is served by many international carriers.

▶ **Best Time to Visit:** The austral summer—December through March—sees the warmest weather and is the most popular time to visit. Whale watching is at its peak in June and July.

▶ **Campgrounds:** There are three campgrounds in Booderee. Bristol Point and Cave Beach require campers to walk in a brief distance; Green Patch can accommodate caravans/RVs. Amenities include potable water, flush toilets, showers, a sheltered cooking area with gas barbecues, and wood barbecues. Peak-season campsites range from $12 to $49 (AUD), with a fee of $11 per adult ($5 per child). Reservations are recommended for the summer season, and can be made by calling +61 2 4443 0977 or emailing booderee. mail@environment.gov.au.

▶ **Activities:** Swimming, wildlife and botanical-garden viewing, hiking, surfing, fishing, cultural experiences.

ULURU–KATA TJUTA NATIONAL PARK

RECOMMENDED BY **James Baillie**

If you were reared off the island, your list of Australian icons is likely to be populated by kangaroos, koalas, the Sydney Opera House, and, if you're old enough, Crocodile Dundee. But if you're a native Aussie, you're more likely to identify with the massive sandstone edifice of Uluru, sometimes called Ayers Rock. "Put simply, Uluru is entirely of Australia and its first people," said James Baillie. "It is hard to put into words the spirituality of Uluru and the connections that have existed between it and the people for thousands of years. There's an instinctive link that the Anangu [the Aboriginal people of the area] share with their land: the stories of creation and cultural learning as well as significant sites. The *Tjukurpa*—which for the Anangu people is both the law and lore of everyday life, defining heritage, relationships, and philosophies—is a deep and complex spiritual system. When you visit Uluru, you're allowed a vivid glimpse into the Anangu life."

Uluru rests in the southern section of Australia's northern territory, near the continent's geographic center. Reaching a maximum height of 1,143 feet, with a circumference of almost six miles, it stands in jarring contrast to the flat and unforgiving environs of Australia's outback; it's now contained within 310,000-acre Uluru-Kata Tjuta National Park. Archaeological research suggests human habitation in the vicinity of Uluru for more than 10,000 years; the Anangu believe that their people have been here much longer. According to *Tjukurpa*, nothing existed before the Anangu's ancestors traveled this land; they formed the trees, the rocks, the water holes; and these features are proof that these acts of creation took place. Beyond its hulking size and spiritual importance, Uluru also draws both humans and other animals for the springs and water holes secreted in its sandstone reaches. Kata Tjuta, a group of thirty-six domed rock formations roughly

DESTINATION 7

fifteen miles west of Uluru, also has great significance for the Anangu. It's considered the center of knowledge.

One of the great thrills of visiting Uluru is the chance to watch the shifting lights and colors upon the sandstone as the sun travels the sky. The play of light is most expressive at sunrise and sunset, and camping in the vicinity of the monolith is the best way to experience this natural spectacle. A conventional camping experience awaits at Ayers Rock Resort; a one-of-a-kind "glamping" (glamor camping) extravaganza is available at Longitude 131°. Here, near the park's border, fifteen luxury tents sit atop red sand dunes. While technically tents, these abodes rival many fine hotel rooms. Each tent comes outfitted with a king bed (or two twins), crisp white linen, an en-suite bathroom with a rain shower, climate control, and wireless internet, among other amenities. Perhaps the best feature of each tent is floor-to-ceiling windows that showcase the changing faces of Uluru. "Guests often choose to spend a leisurely morning watching the sun rise over Uluru without leaving their tent," James continued. "It's an unforgettable experience to lie in bed and witness the day's awakening as darkness slips like a blanket off the giant monolith, revealing its vibrant, earthy colors. Sundowners [drinks] atop the Longitude 131° Dune House (the tent camp's social center) is the ideal way to end the day, with three-hundred-and-sixty-degree views of the surroundings, including Uluru, Kata Tjuta, and the Petermann Ranges."

There are a number of ways to interact with Uluru and Kata Tjuta—and by extension, the Anangu people. For starters, you can visit the cultural center on-site. The two buildings were designed to represent two significant ancestral figures: Kuniya, the python woman, and Liru, the poisonous snake man. While hiking on Uluru is strongly discouraged, a number of walks are available around the landmark. The six-mile base walk lets you take in this immense edifice from all angles, as well as a sample of the region's ecosystems, from acacia woodlands to grassed claypans. (An early start is encouraged.) A shorter walk takes you into Kantju Gorge, where the Mala people (ancestors of the Anangu) are believed to have camped when they first arrived here. Here, there are excellent examples of Aboriginal rock paintings. Park employees provide some tours of Uluru, as well as Kata Tjuta and Walpa Gorge; many more in-depth interpretive tours are provided by concessionaires. For example, guests of Longitude 131° have the option of visiting Kantju Gorge after other visitors have departed, in the moments before sunset. The wave of silence and the sight of the gorge's walls blazing with the last light of the day makes this a touchstone experience . . . especially while enjoying sparkling wine and canapés. Sunrise walks are also offered.

A fitting way to cap off your "glamping" experience at Uluru is a starlight dinner. Guests are spirited to a sand dune overlooking both Uluru and Kata Tjuta, where sundowners and hors d'oeuvres can be enjoyed while watching the dance of colors as the sun sets. From the dune, you're brought to a spot in the desert where torchlit tables are set with white linens. A four-course dinner follows, complemented with a variety of Australian wines. When dinner is finished, the cooking fires and torches are extinguished, and you're left to marvel at the stunning constellations of the southern sky.

JAMES BAILLIE is a twenty-year veteran of high-profile Australian luxury-lodge properties. He was the founding managing director for P&O Resorts in 1998 and steered Australia's first portfolio of premium experiential properties, including Lizard, Bedarra, and Wilson Islands and Silky Oaks Lodge. In 2004, James and his wife, Hayley, opened Capella Lodge on Lord Howe Island, and in 2008 they launched the much-lauded Southern Ocean Lodge on Kangaroo Island. In 2013, James and Hayley acquired Longitude 131°. Throughout his career, James has actively promoted Australia as an upmarket global destination for discerning travelers.

If You Go

▶ **Getting There:** Visitors can fly into Yulara from Sydney on Jetstar (866-397-8170; www.jetstar.com) and through Alice Springs on Qantas Air (800-227-4500; www.qantas.com.au).

▶ **Best Time to Visit:** The weather is cooler in the Aussie fall and winter, between May and September.

▶ **Campgrounds:** Longitude 131° (+61 02 9918 4355; www.longitude131.com.au) offers upscale "glamping" accommodations. Ayers Rock Resort (+61 8 8957 7001; www.ayersrockresort.com.au) offers a host of camping options, from tents to cabins.

▶ **Activities:** Hiking, sightseeing, cultural tours.

CRADLE MOUNTAIN–LAKE ST. CLAIR NATIONAL PARK

RECOMMENDED BY **Jeff Woodward**

The Australian state of Tasmania rests some 150 miles south of Melbourne across the Bass Strait; it's sometimes called "the island off the island." One third larger than Switzerland, Tasmania is considered the most mountainous island of its size in the world. It boasts some of the best-preserved temperate rain forests left on the planet. The coastline is stunning, with myriad coves, bays, beaches, estuaries, and spectacular cliffs. Tasmania is also home to many of Australia's unique mammals, birds, and alpine plants. (Those whose exposure to Tasmania has been limited to the Tasmanian Devil character from Warner Bros. Looney Tunes cartoons may be surprised to learn that such an animal does indeed exist; it's a carnivorous marsupial the size of a smallish dog that poses no danger to humans.)

A visit to Cradle Mountain–Lake St. Clair National Park is one of the best ways to experience the natural wonders of Tasmania. "For me, the great appeal of the park is its ruggedness," said Jeff Woodward. "You can do a morning walk and feel like you've gotten a chance to experience a wild place."

Cradle Mountain–Lake St. Clair National Park occupies 623 square miles in the north-west quadrant of Tasmania. There are two main entrances to the park, one in the south near Lake St. Clair, the other in the north in the shadow of 5,069-foot Cradle Mountain; the north sees considerably more visitors, many of whom are drawn here for the chance to look upon Tasmania's most iconic mountain. (Chance is the operative word here; one moment the weather might be warm and sunny, the next windy and rainy, or even snowy.) The park is the site of one of the world's most celebrated hikes, the Overland Track, a forty-mile tramp that runs north to south through the heart of the park. While the five- or six-day hike may be the best way to experience the Tasmanian Wilderness World Heritage

OPPOSITE:
Cradle Mountain,
the icon of
the Tasmanian
Wilderness World
Heritage Area,
vividly reflected
in Dove Lake.

Area, day-trippers have many opportunities to be exposed to Cradle Mountain–Lake St. Clair's special flora and fauna. "The park's most iconic walk, by far, is the Dove Lake Circuit," Jeff continued. "The track is well formed and suitable for people of all ages. The two-hour walk takes you along the shores of Dove Lake and gives you the iconic view of Cradle Mountain. The trail also takes you through a fine example of our boreal forest." The park's exquisite flora includes pandani (which resembles pandanus palms, but is a unique species endemic to Tasmania), eucalyptus, and pencil pines; some of the pencil pines can live one thousand years or more.

"Another fantastic walk that's accessible for most people is the Cradle Valley Boardwalk," Jeff shared. "It takes you from the Interpretation Center down to Ronny Creek, two and a half or three miles total. There's not much up and down, and there are some great mountain views. You can continue on to Dove Lake from this walk. If you get a nice day and desire a more rigorous hike, consider a walk to Marion's Lookout, which is the first good vantage point on the plateau leading to the summit of Cradle Mountain. In fact, you can get some views similar to what you'd get from the summit. If you continue past Marion's Lookout another twenty minutes, you reach a second overlook that opens up all the views looking south. You're able to see much of the terrain that would be covered if you were hiking the Overland Track."

There are no campgrounds in Cradle Mountain–Lake St. Clair National Park; use of shelters along the route of the Overland Track is reserved primarily for through-hikers. Cradle Mountain Tourist Park and Campground rests just north of the park. While drinking water is limited, some sites with hookups are available, and there are cooking shelters, should the skies open up. Another rustic option is one of the cabins at the Waldheim Chalet, which rests roughly three miles inside the park. Originally built in 1912 by Kate and Gustav Weindorfer (early champions of the region's designation as a national park), the original Waldheim (German for "forest home") Chalet was pulled down for safety reasons in the late 1970s, but rebuilt using traditional bush carpentry techniques. Though simple, the cabins include heat, basic cooking utensils, and an electric stove. (Showers and flush toilets reside in a separate structure.)

Australia's endemic fauna is certainly an attraction for anyone visiting the park. Kangaroos will not be encountered, but many other special animals are present. Wombats are common, especially near the start of the track, as are pademelons (another smaller relative of the kangaroo) and Bennett's wallabies. Tasmanian devils are not common on the trail, but Tasmania's native cat, the quoll, is very active in the evening, hunting small prey. Though rarely encountered, platypuses are also present in Cradle Mountain–Lake St. Clair. Perhaps the most enigmatic of Australia's roster of incredible creatures, platypuses appear like a fusion of otter (furry body) and duck (striking bill and webbed feet).

Note: there is a Tasmanian devil sanctuary near the park, Devils@Cradle, where an encounter with this carnivorous marsupial is guaranteed.

JEFF WOODWARD has been a park ranger at Cradle Mountain–Lake St. Clair National Park for almost four years. He spent his first seven months as an Overland Track ranger, spending eight days at a time walking sections of the Overland Track checking passes, assisting walkers, and performing general maintenance on the infrastructure. For the last three years, he has been based at Cradle Mountain, working as an interpretation ranger/visitor services officer. Prior to working at Cradle, Jeff spent ten years as a tour guide in the Northern Territory. He is a keen bushwalker and climber, and when he's not "out bush," enjoys spending time with his wife and two daughters and playing music.

If You Go

▶ **Getting There:** The nearest major airport to the north entrance of the park is in Launceston, which is served from Sydney and Melbourne by Qantas Air (800-227-4500; www.qantas.com). There is bus service from Launceston via Tassielink (www.tassielink.com.au).

▶ **Best Time to Visit:** November through May, with the late austral summer and early fall seeing the most stable weather.

▶ **Campgrounds:** There are no campgrounds in the park, and shelters are reserved for Overland Track hikers. However, there is a campground near the north entrance: Cradle Mountain Tourist Park and Campground (+61 6492 1395; www.discoveryholidayparks.com.au) has tent sites for $25 to $30 (AUD). Simple structures—the Waldheim Chalet cabins—are available for rent within the park (+61 6491 2271); a cabin for four is $95 (AUD).

▶ **Activities:** Hiking, fishing, wildlife viewing.

BELIZE FOUNDATION FOR RESEARCH AND ENVIRONMENTAL EDUCATION

RECOMMENDED BY **Jacob Marlin**

Sometimes a camping adventure provides a chance to retreat from the demands of your everyday routine to reflect on your life. For Jacob Marlin, a camping trip to the Maya Mountains of southern Belize completely changed the course of his life.

"Growing up, I was completely taken by the natural world, and loved reptiles and amphibians," Jacob began. "In college, I studied biology and decided that someday I wanted to dedicate myself to rain forest conservation. During college I spent some time in Belize and fell in love with the country and its people. After college, I took a few different jobs around the States, working with reptiles, trying to pay bills while figuring out how I could pursue my dream. In 1993, I was invited by an explorer friend of mine to join an expedition to the Bladen Nature Reserve to take a reptile/amphibian inventory of the region. [The nearly 100,000-acre reserve, which rests on the southeast flank of the Maya Mountains, is among the most biodiversity-rich areas in Central America; combined with contiguous protected areas, it comprises one of the largest intact swaths of rain forest north of the Amazon.] When we reached the area after four days of bushwhacking, I was blown away. There were undisturbed Mayan ruins, caves full of pottery and abundant wildlife. You had the sense that no humans had been here for a very long time; it was that pristine. After the trip, I felt like I'd found a place where I could get involved."

It took a few more years, but Jacob eventually found some land at the gateway to the reserve and scraped together enough resources to make his dream a reality. Today, people can experience the pristine rain forest of southern Belize at the Belize Foundation for Research and Environmental Education (BFREE), a scientific field station that welcomes curious visitors of all types.

OPPOSITE:
The Bladen branch of the Monkey River flows through BFREE en route to the Caribbean.

51

Most Belizean visitors are drawn to the coastal regions and the attractions of the Mesoamerican Barrier Reef, which stretches along the entire coast. But given that much of its original rain forest is intact, Belize's interior is seeing increasing ecotourism activity. Several high-end lodges (like Chaa Creek) provide a more pampered jungle experience. While the amenities may be more modest at BFREE, the access to Belize's rain forest wonders is just as impressive. "The 1,150-acre property has an extensive trail network through a variety of habitats," Jacob explained. "The life blood of the area is the Bladen River [technically the Bladen branch of the Monkey River], which flows out of the Maya Mountains through BFREE. It's so clean, you can drink from it while you're swimming. And it's so clear, you feel as though you're drifting in an aquarium. Nearby there's an oxbow lagoon that's home to nesting Morelet's crocodiles as well as agami and boat-billed herons. We have a 112-foot-tall observation tower that takes you into the forest canopy to observe some of the 350 species of birds that have been recorded here, as well as black howler monkeys. Many larger mammals—tapir, jaguar, ocelot, margay and puma—are seen at BFREE. The coffee and cacao farm is a great place to see cats and tapir at night, as the understory is not as dense as you find in the wild forest, and there are trails throughout."

A camping trip to BFREE begins with a six-mile ride (or walk, in the rainy season) up the Bladen Nature Reserve entrance road. There's no camp store at the other end, so you'll need to bring all your gear. Eventually you'll reach the Bladen River; the BFREE compound is on the other side, with the Maya Mountains rising in the distance. If a canoe isn't waiting and the river is flowing clear, you can wade or swim across and grab a canoe and paddle back across to pick up your gear. (Calling ahead is recommended so someone can be there to assist.) There's no strictly defined campground once you reach BFREE; most campers choose to pitch their tent by the river. Such a site provides an ideal vantage point from which to spy wildlife heading to the river to drink at dusk. Some might opt for a hammock with requisite mosquito netting. (A simple bunkhouse is also available with twenty-four beds provided in four rooms.) Meals are prepared communally and served in a thatched-roof dining room. Showers (serviced by a rainwater collection system) are available in the bunkhouse.

While exploring the rain forest environs of BFREE and Bladen Nature Reserve on your own will be an eye-opening experience, it's even more fulfilling to tour the area with someone who understands the intricacies of this fecund ecosystem. Most of the staff members at BFREE are local Mayans who have expertise in different areas—from ornithology to making chocolate—and are happy to share their wisdom. BFREE offers field courses on the flora and fauna of the region with resident and guest biologists throughout the year. Courses combine lectures, guided hikes and participation in some of the scientific projects underway at the foundation. Participants need no formal scientific background, just a passion for the outdoors.

JACOB MARLIN found a passion for the natural world at a young age, with a focus on reptiles and amphibians. In his early twenties, Jacob traveled to Belize to explore the country and its wild places—soon after, he co-founded and established the Belize Foundation for Research and Environmental Education (BFREE). The nonprofit's mission is to conserve the biodiversity and cultural heritage of Belize, primarily through its work at a biological field station in southern Belize. Jacob is an active advocate for the conservation and protection of the Bladen Nature Reserve and the larger system of National Protected Areas in Belize. He is an adjunct assistant professor at University of North Carolina Wilmington.

If You Go

▶ **Getting There:** International travelers reach Belize via Belize City, which is served by a number of carriers. Most will take either the Southern Transport or James Bus Line south to the entrance road, or fly to Independence via Maya Island Air (501-223-1140; www.mayaislandair.com) and take a taxi to the field station.

▶ **Best Time to Visit:** February through mid-May provides milder temperatures and drier conditions. November through January is prime time for birding; if you're interested in reptiles and amphibians, visit in June and July.

▶ **Campground:** Belize Foundation for Research and Environmental Education (+501.671.1299; www.bfreebz.org) can accommodate tent campers and also offers basic lodging. Foundation employees are available for interpretive hikes and meals are provided. Campsites begin at $15; meals are provided at $10, $12, $13 for breakfast, lunch, and dinner, respectively. A one-time conservation fee of $15 is charged to all visitors.

▶ **Activities:** Wildlife viewing, hiking, swimming, canoeing, environmental education.

ABU CAMP

RECOMMENDED BY **Grant Woodrow**

Abu Camp is not your typical camp. First, it can only be reached by plane. Second, the tents more closely resemble five-star hotel rooms than your average Coleman or Kelty. And finally, your fellow "campers" are elephants.

"For me, it's not just the isolated location in the Okavango Delta, or the luxury of the camp itself, or the presence of the elephants that makes Abu special," began Grant Woodrow. "It's really the mix of it all. Though the chance to have such intimate, personalized experiences with the elephants certainly makes Abu different than other safari camps."

Abu Camp is a 400,000-acre private reserve in the Okavango Delta, an immense inland delta formed where the Okavango River meets the Kalahari Desert in north-western Botswana, a country just north of South Africa. The wetland sanctuary that flourishes here—an immense series of lagoons, channels, and palm-filled islands—supports a wide assortment of plains game, including zebra, impala, tsessebe (a species of antelope), wildebeest, buffalo, warthogs, leopards, cheetahs, and lions. Five hundred bird species also call the Okavango home. There are herds of wild elephants ranging the Okavango, but Abu Camp has its own herd: Cathy, Lorato, Sherini, Warona, Naledi, and Paseka. How the elephants came to Abu Camp is fodder for a feel-good Hollywood movie; indeed, Hollywood does play into the story. Back in the early 1970s, Randall Moore, the founder of Abu Camp, had joined a little husband/wife circus act in Washington state and began to look after the circus's three elephants. When the husband (Morgan Berry) died, Moore learned that he had inherited the elephants. Moore decided to return the elephants back to their natural homeland and rehabilitate them in the African wild. After successfully reintroducing the elephants to the Pilanesberg Game Reserve in South Africa, Moore was asked to find three more elephants to star in

OPPOSITE:
Guests at Abu
Camp enjoy
the chance to
see the African
bush through the
eyes of resident
elephants.

the movie *Circles in a Forest*. He returned from America with Abu, Benny, and Cathy, but once the movie was finished, he was not permitted to reintroduce them into the reserve where the movie was shot. That was when the idea of the elephant-back safari struck Moore. The government of Botswana recognized the potential of the idea, and Moore (and his pachyderm protégés) relocated.

Abu Camp is not the end of the road for the elephants. The goal of Abu Camp is to return previously captive elephants to the wild. "The Abu elephants can move around the bush pretty much at will," Grant continued. "If they show a willingness to return to the wild they can." When members of the Abu herd do return to the wild, researchers from Elephants Without Borders monitor their progress in acclimatizing to their freedom.

When guests arrive at Abu Camp they are introduced to each elephant and briefed on the animal's background and personality. But your real introduction comes the next day, when you have the chance to spend the morning with the elephants on a walk. Each elephant has a handler—a *mahout*—who rides on the elephant's neck, with his legs behind the animal's ears. The elephants have a saddle of sorts behind the mahout, and that's where you sit. "Many guests choose to walk alongside the elephants," Grant explained. "Walking provides a great perspective to observe and even feel what an elephant does. It's like you've become part of the herd." Each morning, guides take a different route through the wetlands. Whether you ride or walk with the elephants, you're able to get much closer to the wildlife than you would in a Range Rover. Giraffes, kudu, zebras, and hippos are regularly encountered; big cats are not a guarantee, but they are certainly present. (If you prefer a more traditional safari experience, game drives in a vehicle and guided *mokoro* [dugout canoe] paddles on the delta are available.)

The six canvas tents at Abu Camp are elevated upon wooden decking and overlook the nearby lagoon. Each tent has wood floors, mahogany sleigh-style beds, and spacious en-suite bathrooms with a large outdoor bath overlooking the stunning panorama. The husband and wife that run the lodge create a friendly house-party atmosphere. There are sundowners around a fire before dinner, and excellent wine with dinner. Guests drift to sleep surrounded by the sounds of the bush, the calls of nightjars and owls, and perhaps even the growls from a local pride of lions. "There are no fences around Abu Camp," Grant said. "We have wild animals coming through the camp daily. You're part of the environment here. I like to say we have a twenty-four-hour safari experience that allows you to disconnect from daily routines."

Guests at Abu are assured a one-of-a-kind wildlife experience. But they're also part of a larger narrative. "I see the elephants at Abu as ambassadors of the bigger elephant concerns we have in Africa," Grant ventured. "Their plight is drastic. When a visitor has had a chance to walk with the elephants, they're able to take home an amazing story. This story will contribute to the larger cause of elephant conservation."

GRANT WOODROW is managing director of Wilderness Safaris Botswana. He joined Wilderness Safaris in 1996 as an assistant camp manager of Xigera in Botswana's Okavango Delta and went on to manage other Botswana camps. Grant has a BS in zoology and an honors degree in wildlife management. He has always had a passion for wildlife and the environment, and this led to him developing the Botswana Environmental Division in 2000. In this role, he had the opportunity to manage various ecological projects, including the reintroduction of rhino into the Okavango Delta. His work on company environmental minimum standards set a benchmark for future standards within the tourism industry in Botswana. Grant worked in various senior operational positions before being appointed managing director of Okavango Wilderness Safaris in 2007.

If You Go

▶ **Getting There:** To reach Abu Camp, you'll need to travel to the town of Maun on Air Botswana (800-518-7781; www.airbotswana.co.bw), which offers service from Johannesburg. From Maun, a charter flight will spirit you to Abu Camp.

▶ **Best Time to Visit:** Peak season is June through October, though Abu is open year-round.

▶ **Campground:** Abu Camp is not exactly a campground; in fact, it's about as glamorous a tent experience as you could hope for. Wilderness Safaris (+27 11 807 1800; www.wilderness-safaris.com) books four-day/three-night stays at Abu Camp.

▶ **Activities:** Interacting with elephants, wildlife viewing.

PACIFIC RIM NATIONAL PARK RESERVE

RECOMMENDED BY **Barb Brittain**

Pacific Rim National Park Reserve is three parks in one, spread over 126,500 acres along the southwestern coast of Vancouver Island in British Columbia. The Long Beach Unit—the section of the park of greatest interest to the car camper—is a 34,800-acre swath of land sandwiched between the Vancouver Island Range and the open Pacific. The only section of the park that's explorable by road, the Long Beach Unit boasts its eponymous beach, an expanse of lush coastal temperate rainforest, and a number of sites that speak to the rich history of the Nuu-chah-nulth First Nations people that have long called this region home. The second unit of the park is the Broken Group Islands. This archipelago of one hundred-plus islands and islets scattered throughout Barkley Sound can only be reached by boat . . . usually kayak. The last unit of Pacific Rim is the West Coast Trail, a forty-seven-mile backpacking route through rain forests, along sandstone cliffs and over beaches. There are three entry and exit points for hikers to choose from, allowing them to explore as little or as much of the trail as they like.

"Green Point is consistently voted one of the best campgrounds in Canada," Barb Brittain began. "It's smack-dab in the middle of the Long Beach Unit. You're in the center of Long Beach, a ten-mile stretch of fine, silvery sand. The campground is nestled into the temperate rainforest, where light filters through the moss and lichen that hang from the trees; from some sites, you can see the open Pacific below. Even if you can't, you're only a five- or ten-minute walk from the beach, where you have one of the best sunsets in Canada. Many campers use Green Point as a base for exploring the Pacific. Those with younger children will don wetsuits and go boogie boarding; families with older children will don wetsuits and go surfing. (Surf lessons are available from concessionaires just outside the park.) Green Point has an amphitheater, and most nights in the summer there are

OPPOSITE: The Nuu-cha-nulth Trail weaves through thick forest and ends at Florence Beach.

interpretive programs, some which focus on First Nations storytelling to how (and how not) to interact with Pacific Rim's other inhabitants—cougars, wolves, and black bears. Both drive-in and walk-in sites are available. Beginning in 2014, we began offering 'Equipped Camping.' We provide campers with a four- to six-person tent, sleeping pads, a stove, and a lantern. They just need to bring food, cookware, and sleeping bags."

A must for anyone visiting the Long Beach Unit is the Kwisitis Visitor Center. Set above Wickaninnish Beach, it includes detailed exhibits highlighting the natural and cultural history of the area. Members of the Nuu-chah-nulth communities were very involved in developing the content that would be shared in the Visitor Center. Campers can join guided interpretive walks in the summer months to learn more about Nuu-chah-nulth culture, the ocean, and rain forest.

Pacific Rim attracts paddlers from around the world, and no wonder; a kayak is an ideal platform for exploring this rich coastal ecosystem. For the more adventurous, there's the option of camping at one of the seven designated campgrounds in the park's Broken Group Islands Unit. "You have to bring your own water and be pretty self-sufficient," Barb advised, "but it can be a wonderful experience. The islands have very different habitats. Gibraltar and Hand Islands are at the back of Barkley Sound, and thus are easier to reach, have calmer water, and are often in the sun. The outer islands like Clarke and Gilbert are more exposed and can be fogged over—though for experienced kayakers, it's stunning paddling. [Tour companies in Tofino and Ucluelet can provide kayaks, and guided trips are available.] There are many kayaking options for day-trippers too. An easy half-day paddle is in Grice Bay, toward Tofino. It's an inlet with lots of little, narrow fingers. You have to be sure to go during high tide, or else you can get grounded. In the summer, gray whales sometimes come into the bay to feed. I've had whales come right under my boat as they work their way through."

Pacific Rim National Park Reserve recently inaugurated the Long Beach Challenge, a scenic run (or walk or jog) along a roughly six-mile stretch of Long Beach. There's no set time to tackle the run; participants purchase a challenge time card and embark on the beach on their own schedule. A monitoring system will detect when you begin and end the course. "My daughter and I started running together years ago to help strengthen her lungs, as she has asthma," Barb recalled. "Usually we run a half hour in the morning. Last November, we decided to do the challenge, though it would be longer than our usual run. We got up just before dawn, and it was still dark when we got to the beach. It was low tide—the best time to run, as the sand is hard and a creek you need to cross is at a fordable level. The sky was stunning as we began, with the clouds above capturing the bright red of the sunrise in the east. The beautiful red of the clouds was reflected back in the water, so we had sunrise above us and below us. As we made our way through sea foam, across creeks, past dunes, and around rocks, we were heading into the daylight, with the gradient changing from black to red to full sunshine as we reached the finish."

BARB BRITTAIN grew up in nearby Port Alberni and spent much time exploring Vancouver Island's west coast with family and friends, walking the beaches, hiking the trails, and paddling through the islands and lakes. She started working for Parks Canada in 1985 and has spent most of her career at Pacific Rim National Park Reserve, where she has worked in a wide variety of visitor support roles. Living in Ucluelet has allowed Barb to continue sharing her love of the area with family, friends, and park visitors.

If You Go

▶ **Getting There:** Most distant visitors fly into Vancouver or Victoria and then drive to Pacific Rim (five hours from Victoria; three and a half hours from Nanaimo, where the ferry from Vancouver drops you). Another option is to fly to Tofino–Long Beach Airport, which is served by Orca Airways (888-359-6722; www.flyorcaair.com) and KD Air (800-665-4244; www.kdair.com).

▶ **Best Time to Visit:** The park is open from early May through mid-October; June through early September is the most popular time to visit.

▶ **Campgrounds:** Green Point (in Long Beach Unit) is Pacific Rim's front-country campground. It has ninety-four drive-in units and twenty walk-in sites; amenities include flush toilets, fire pits, picnic tables, and potable water. RVs are welcome, though no hookups are available. Sites range from $17.60 to $23.50 (CAD); reservations can be made through Parks Canada (877-737-3783; https://reservation.pc.gc.ca).

▶ **Activities:** Boating, hiking, surfing, First Nations cultural experiences.

MOJAVE ROAD

RECOMMENDED BY **Rich Hill**

"There are so many options available when you look to do a trip," Rich Hill opined. "One of the main criteria I use is to find spots where there aren't a lot of people. A few years back I took out a map, and one place not too far from where I live that looked intriguing was Mojave National Preserve. I started doing some research, and a video of this dad and his daughter driving across the preserve in an antique Land Rover popped up. They were on a dirt path called the Mojave Road. It took three days for them to head across the preserve from east to west. I didn't need to hear much else."

Mojave National Preserve is a bastion of serenity between the somewhat less tranquil metropolises of Las Vegas and Los Angeles. At 1.6 million acres, it's the third-largest unit of the National Park System in the Lower 48, its high desert environs encompassing vast sand dunes (the Kelso Dunes reach heights of 650 feet), mountains (reaching almost 8,000 feet), Joshua tree forests, and volcanic remnants (like the Cinder Cone Lava Beds). In late winter/early spring, visitors can generally count on expanses of wildflowers summoned forth by winter rains. To take in all the preserve has to offer would require a number of visits; but a drive across the preserve's expanses via the Mojave Road will provide tremendous exposure to many of the treasures the preserve has to offer.

The Mojave Road stretches 138 miles, beginning near the west bank of the Colorado River at the Nevada/Arizona border in the east and bisecting the preserve until its end at Camp Cady. For much of its course, the road is little different than it was in the days when Mojave Indians used the route to reach the coast. (The path was likely chosen thanks to the presence of water at several points.) Discovered by Franciscan priest/explorer Francisco Garcés in 1776, the path was one of several options for westward immigrants. With the discovery of gold in the north in the 1840s, it became less significant for pioneers.

OPPOSITE:
The Mojave
Road is a dream
come true for
"overlanders,"
four-wheel drive
enthusiasts who
prize self-reliance
during their
travels.

(Its popularity wasn't enhanced by reports of tribal attacks, by the Chemehuevi and Paiute peoples further west along the road, and difficult terrain—considerable stretches of sand and steep passes inhospitable to wagon trains.) Still, the Mojave Road was used as a freight and mail route, and by the 1860s, several forts were established along the way to support trade. Remains of these outposts are preserved today, as is the site of the old railroad station at Kelso.

Driving rough trails through the wilderness and sleeping in or alongside a vehicle may not be everyone's idea of a relaxing camping trip, but this mode of travel—overlanding—has a modest though passionate following. *Overland Journal* defines overlanding as:

> . . . self-reliant adventure travel to remote destinations where the journey is the primary goal. Typically, but not exclusively, accommodated by mechanized off-highway capable transport (from bicycles to trucks), where the principal form of lodging is camping; often lasting for extended lengths of time (months to years) and often spanning international boundaries. Technical terrain can be encountered throughout the journey, and the travelers may even seek out the most challenging route to a destination as part of their experience, but overland travel is not the same as recreational "fourwheeling," where the primary objective is overcoming challenging obstacles.

The preferred vehicle for early overlanders was the Land Rover, first made available in 1948; it remains popular today. "In our three-vehicle convoy, there were two Toyotas (Land Cruiser and 4Runner) and one Jeep," Rich added. "Though we camped each night, it certainly felt more like we were traveling than camping."

There are several official campgrounds within the Mojave National Preserve—Hole-in-the-Wall (named for the sculptured rock walls that surround the area) and Mid Hills. Both offer potable water and pit toilets. Overlanders set up at less formal sites along the road. "The park service likes you to camp at spots that have been used repeatedly by other travelers over the years," Rich explained. "We had a guide book [Dennis Casebier's *Mojave Road Guide*] that highlights these spots. The first night of our adventure we found one of these spots; the second, we hunted for a while, but eventually just pulled off the trail. Traffic certainly wasn't a problem—over three days, we came upon one other vehicle and one couple that was camping.

"There are a few things that have stayed with me about my Mojave Road trip. First, it was the incredible variety of the terrain. The first day, we were at a higher elevation, enveloped by pinyon pines and incredible rock formations. On the second day, we descended to lower-elevation desert territory. For long stretches, there's absolutely nothing, just sand. Then suddenly you come into a stretch of black volcanic sand and immense lava pillars. That second night, there were the most amazing stars. On the third day, the topography changes drastically again, as you head over an expansive salt flat. All told, there were five or six completely different terrain changes. Everyone in my group loved the element of surprise the Mojave Road provided. You just didn't know what would be around the corner. The other thing that's stayed with me is the isolation of the place. It's rare these days to feel so alone."

RICH HILL has more than twenty years' experience in the specialty outdoor industry, ranging from white-water river guide to a front-office executive. He's been able to work with great brands like Kelty, Marmot, Patagonia, and prAna, and each has provided a unique perspective and opportunity to enjoy the outdoors. From his home in Ventura, California, Rich is currently working on his new car-camping concept called Ticla (www.ticla.com), a brand designed to reenergize the sleepy camping-equipment marketplace with some fresh ideas and a sense of style.

If You Go

► **Getting There:** Las Vegas is the closest major airport, roughly sixty miles east of the preserve. Four-wheel-drive SUVs are available at a number of rental car agencies.

► **Best Time to Visit:** The preserve is open year-round, though during the summer, daytime temperatures can reach well over one hundred degrees. Spring and fall temperatures are more moderate.

► **Campgrounds:** There are two first-come, first-served campgrounds in the preserve, Hole-in-the-Wall and Mid Hills; group camping is available at Black Canyon Equestrian & Group Campground, which accepts reservations by calling 760-928-2572. Guidelines for roadside camping can be found at www.nps.gov/moja.

► **Activities:** Overlanding, four-wheeling, hiking, hunting (in fall).

JULIA PFEIFFER BURNS STATE PARK

RECOMMENDED BY **Phil Bergman**

"We see many visitors from all over the country, and from overseas too," Ranger Phil Bergman began. "They often ask where they will find Big Sur, as if it were a specific piece of land. While there is a town of Big Sur, the phrase—"Big South"—refers to the coastline from Carmel in the north to San Simeon in the south. That's nearly ninety miles of relatively undeveloped land along the center of the California coast."

But a few minutes along this rugged coastline make it easy to understand why visitors travel so far to get to Big Sur. Here, the Santa Lucia Mountains rise abruptly by the Pacific and misty valleys shelter forests of giant redwoods, creating some of North America's most iconic coastal vistas. One can only imagine how deeply real estate moguls have longed to monetize these views; yet the hardy terrain through much of this stretch has made development unfeasible. Indeed, it wasn't until Highway 1 was constructed (between 1919 and 1937) that Big Sur began to enter the broader national consciousness. Today, the stretch of road running through Big Sur is considered one of the crown jewels of the American National Scenic Byways system. The beauty and isolation of Big Sur has attracted many writers since its discovery, ranging from Robinson Jeffers and Henry Miller to Jack Kerouac and Richard Brautigan. Their musings on the place no doubt further burnished its reputation.

There are a number of campgrounds along the northern section of the Big Sur coast, including the three state parks that Phil helps oversee; beginning in the north, these are Andrew Molera, Pfeiffer Big Sur, and Julia Pfeiffer Burns. He described each in detail. "The campground at Andrew Molera is set in an open field that's about two-thirds of a mile from the beach. You have to hike your gear in about one quarter mile to reach one of twenty-four sites. Though you have to hike in, the campground has decent amenities—

OPPOSITE:
The vista of
McWay Falls
at Julia Pfeiffer
Burns State Park
is one of the most
photographed
settings in
Big Sur.

67

Most of Yosemite's attractions were hewn by Mother Nature, but at least one was made by man—the grand Ahwahnee Hotel, considered a masterpiece of "parkitecture." "The Ahwahnee was built in 1927 to house prominent people who were invited to the park in hopes of attracting funding," Kari explained. "After all, these sorts of people weren't going to camp! Some visitors don't realize that the Ahwahnee is open to the public, even if you don't have a reservation. Anyone can visit the common rooms, including the Great Lounge with its huge fireplaces. Be sure to visit the Grand Dining Room. Every time I go in, I can't help but think of the dining room at Hogwarts in the Harry Potter movies, with its hanging lanterns."

KARI COBB has been a park ranger in Yosemite National Park since 2004. She graduated from the University of California at Santa Cruz in 2007 with a BA in sociology and a minor in legal studies. She furthered her education at Fresno State in Fresno, California, by obtaining an MS in criminology in 2009. When she's not at work, you will find her hiking in the Yosemite backcountry, looking for the next secret spot of solitude.

If You Go

▶ **Getting There:** The Fresno Yosemite International Airport is roughly two and a half hours to Yosemite Valley and is served by many airlines, including Alaska Airlines (800-252-7522; www.alaskaair.com) and American Airlines (800-433-7300; www.aa.com). Yosemite is approximately four hours from Bay Area airports.

▶ **Best Time to Visit:** Yosemite is open year-round, though snow often covers the high country until late May. Summers boast the best weather (and crowds); early fall can be a great time to visit.

▶ **Campgrounds:** Yosemite has thirteen campgrounds; seven are served by a reservation system, the others are first come, first served. Slots fill up early. Visit www.nps.gov/yose for an overview of sites; visit www.recreation.gov or call 877-444-6777 for reservations.

▶ **Activities:** Hiking, fishing, biking, horseback riding, rock climbing, rafting/kayaking, and ranger tours.

OPPOSITE:
The grandeur of Yosemite Valley is almost too good to be true.

14
DESTINATION

TORRES DEL PAINE NATIONAL PARK

RECOMMENDED BY **Stefan Urlaub**

Stefan Urlaub still vividly recalls setting foot in Torres del Paine National Park. "I'd had a long journey to reach southern Chilean Patagonia, and seeing the Torres (the park's eponymous mountain range) for the first time was one of the most magical moments of my life. Like a flow moment of unity with nature, I felt proud of being part of this wonder called Earth." Stefan's not alone in his admiration; National Geographic has called Torres del Paine the fifth-most-beautiful place in the world.

Like Texas, Patagonia is as much a state of mind as a place. Encompassing roughly 400,000 square miles of seemingly endless steppes, groaning glaciers, spiky pink granite peaks, and electric-blue lakes, wind-pummeled Patagonia—divided between Chile and Argentina across the bottom of South America—is still very much a frontier. (The border between the countries in the region continues to be amorphous, furthering Patagonia's reputation as a place where one can melt into the landscape.) Torres del Paine National Park, at the southern tip of the Andes in the region of Magallanes, combines all the natural wonders Patagonia is known for in its 935 square miles. A number of famed trekking routes wind among the park's glaciers, lakes, and mountains, including the W Trek and the Paine Circuit. But you needn't strap on a backpack to experience the park's wonders. Several campgrounds host visitors . . . and you'll also find a unique "glamping" venue to use as a base camp from which to explore the park via day excursions—EcoCamp Patagonia.

EcoCamp combines a premium location—overlooking the three iconic granitic spires of Torres del Paine (South, Central, and North)—with the novelty of geodesic domes as living structures. "Visitors can appreciate the Torres at sunrise as they wake up and again at sunset as they return after a day's trek," Stefan continued. "No journey time is needed to start trekking, guests step out of their dome and pick up the trail leading to the Torres

OPPOSITE:
Visitors to
EcoCamp
Patagonia enjoy
"glamping" in
specially designed
geodesic domes.

or along the Los Cuernos path. EcoCamp's dome design was inspired by the Kaweskars, a group of nomadic Patagonian inhabitants whose presence in Torres del Paine is documented. They arrived by canoe in the fifteenth century and made no demands on natural resources as they traveled from place to place, setting up and dismantling their semicircular huts built from simple materials, leaving no trace behind. To keep warm, they lit fires inside the domes." (The modern notion of geodesic domes was championed in the late 1940s by architect/futurist R. Buckminster Fuller, who valued the domes for their stability and economic use of space.) EcoCamp pioneered the use of geodesic domes for travelers in 1999. Their standard domes keep the at-times-fierce Patagonian wind at bay and feature ceiling windows to take in the southern stars. Like your standard-issue tent, the standard domes lack heat, but an assortment of fleece blankets should keep you cozy. (More ornate domes that include propane heaters and a private bathroom with a composting toilet are also available.) Guests take their meals and socialize in one of the Community Domes, which boast wood stoves, a bar, a library, and an *asado* platform for the preparation of Patagonian lamb barbecues. (This is glamping, after all!)

Though one could be tempted to relax at EcoCamp and take in the views of the Torres, you traveled this far to immerse yourself in Torres del Paine. Stefan described a few favorite day excursions. "One day, you might take a drive to Laguna Azul, a beautiful glacial lake with the Torres looming in the distance. On the way you'll see many guanacos (a small member of the camel family, resembling a llama), one of Torres del Paine's "Big Five" animals; the other four are the Andean condor, South Andean deer, lesser rhea, and puma. At the lake, a Chilean barbeque awaits. As you wander the lake's shores, there's a good chance you'll see condor riding the thermals; their wingspans can exceed nine feet! Pumas are very rarely encountered, but visitors have the option of retaining a safari guide to track these wary cats, so they might catch a glimpse. Another popular day trip takes you to Glacier Grey. Driving to Grey Lake, we're treated to spectacular views of Los Cuernos [The Horns] del Paine and will likely come upon more herds of guanacos. A brief boat ride takes you across the lake to the towering blue walls of Glacier Grey." You won't get too close, however, as the glacier is actively calving.

As noted above, Torres del Paine is a celebrated trekking destination. The W is the park's most renowned circuit, so named because there are five destination points along the way, in the rough shape of a "W." From EcoCamp Patagonia, you're well positioned to hike two legs of the circuit, Valle del Francés (French Valley) and the Towers base. "We drive to Lake Pehoé and take a catamaran to the northwestern shore, where the French Valley trail begins," Stefan described. "It's a steep trail that leads to the heart of the Paine massif. If the group is moving quickly, we can make it all the way to the hanging bridge above the French River, which is at the foot of the south face of the massif. In one direction, there are the fantastic rock formations—Hoja (Blade), Máscara (Mask), Espada (Sword), Catedral (Cathedral), Aleta de Tiburón (Shark's Fin), and Fortaleza (Fortress)—in the other, the entire valley. The hike to the base of Torres del Paine is perhaps my favorite. Whoever comes to this region of Patagonia dreams of seeing the famous towers from their base. We take the path through the Ascencio Valley on the towers' eastern face through beech forests. Reaching the moraine, you must navigate some steep boulders while gaining elevation. Eventually, the towers come into full view, with a glacial lake below. Getting there is an adventure, and reaching the towers makes you feel something special, much more than the sensation of being in the middle of a postcard."

STEFAN URLAUB is a native of Stuttgart, Germany, and now serves as Cascada's communications manager. Stefan loves traveling and adventure and the finer things in life, such as good Chilean wine. A big mountain fan, Stefan enjoys trekking, snowboarding, and mountaineering in Chile and Argentina.

If You Go

▶ **Getting There:** Travelers can reach Torres del Paine National Park via Punta Arenas, which is served by LAN Airlines (866-435-9526; www.lan.com) via Santiago.
▶ **Best Time to Visit:** Torres del Paine National Park is open year-round, though the weather is best during the austral spring and summer—October through March.
▶ **Campgrounds:** EcoCamp Patagonia (800-901-6987; www.ecocamp.travel) offers unique camp-style lodging in geodesic domes and an array of tours around the park. Traditional campgrounds in the area include Lago Pehoé Camping (+56 61 411355), Río Serrano Camping (+56 61 411355), and Laguna Azul Camping (+56 61 411157).
▶ **Activities:** Hiking, wildlife viewing, fly-fishing, and biking.

THE DALMATIAN COAST

RECOMMENDED BY **Adriano Palman**

"If you can imagine a mix of Italy, Spain, and Greece, with a bit of Eastern Europe mixed in, then you have a good idea of Croatia," began Adriano Palman. "One difference is people don't know as much about Croatia as its better-known neighbors. It's a small country, roughly the size of West Virginia. Yet there are so many kinds of landscapes—mountains, coast, canyon country—it's like ten countries in one. Though the inland areas have many appeals, most tourists visit the seaside, especially the Dalmatian Coast."

Many travel-business insiders consider Croatia a hidden gem, combining many of the best aspects of better-known southern European destinations—crystal-clear water, a mild climate, rich culture, and colorful cuisine—without the crowds. The republic rests across the Adriatic Sea from Italy and is bordered by Hungary to the north, Slovenia to the northwest, Serbia to the east, and Montenegro to the southeast; Bosnia and Herzegovina cuts into the center of the country, giving Croatia a horseshoe shape. Croatia has a rich and incredibly complex history; the turbulence that's dogged Croatia stems largely from its location, at the nexus of central, southern, and Eastern Europe. Despite the travails they've faced through the twentieth century, the Croats are by and large a friendly and hospitable people. They work hard, enjoy life, treat visitors well, and are proud of their country and everything it has to offer—which for the outdoor enthusiast is a great deal . . . including fine camping.

"There are campsites literally everywhere on the Croatian coast," Adriano continued. "All the campsites need to meet strict quality standards. ADAC (the German Automobile Club) publishes the bible of campsite guides and ranks each European country for the quality of its camping accommodations. Croatia is currently ranked third." Campgrounds take two basic forms—holiday camps and mini-campsites. The holiday camps can be

OPPOSITE:
The islands
off Croatia's
southeast
coast—Mljet and
Korcula—mix
pristine forests
and picturesque
fishing villages.

79

LAKE DISTRICT NATIONAL PARK

RECOMMENDED BY **Pete Royall**

Whatever your high school or college English class experience with "Tintern Abbey" or "The Prelude," most will agree that William Wordsworth nicely captured the romance and beauty of the Lake District in his poem "Daffodils":

> I wander'd lonely as a cloud
> That floats on high o'er vales and hills,
> When all at once I saw a crowd,
> A host, of golden daffodils;
> Beside the lake, beneath the trees,
> Fluttering and dancing in the breeze.

Pete Royall sums up the appeals of the Lake District with one word: compact. "The park is small enough that you can easily take in all it has to offer," he began, "and a series of trunk routes makes it easy to access most of the region. People hear the phrase Lake District and they picture a plain filled with lakes. Actually, this is the most mountainous area in England. Our ten highest peaks (known as "fells"—an old Norse word from the original Lake District settlers) are here, including Scafell Pike at 3,210 feet. Many people come for the hill walking. The Lake District was sculpted out during the last ice age; the ice left great U-shaped valleys filled with lakes. There are sixteen larger lakes and hundreds of tarns—some great for fishing, some for swimming. Some of the larger lakes have steamer service, so you can see countryside from the water. You can also hire a rowboat or sailboat and go out on your own. The Lake District is a national park, but not in the way that Yellowstone is a national park. It's a working environment, with villages,

OPPOSITE:
Kentmere Valley,
one of many
lake-filled valleys
carved by the last
ice age.

farms, and businesses. [Roughly forty thousand people live within park boundaries.] Life goes on here, though there are rigid restrictions on what sort of development can be undertaken. There are key towns which have been developed to provide tourist facilities such as restaurants, bars, cafés, theaters, and climbing walls, while most of the region's villages are maintained as they were one hundred or two hundred years ago; they're a bit of preserved older England. The valleys seem almost gardenlike, well manicured with ancient, dry-stone walls dividing properties. The hills are a hint of wildness that rise in the background."

The Lake District National Park sits in the northwest corner of England in the county of Cumbria, not far below the Scottish border. The park's 885 square miles have a storybook charm that's underscored by its neat, whitewashed cottages and bucolic fields dotted with sheep, all framed by the ever-present mountains. If Wordsworth's poetry helped romanticize the region, his travelogue—*Guide to the Lakes*—put it on the vacationer's map. Today, the park sees more than twelve million visitors annually. A number come to camp. "Down in the valleys, camping is restricted to established sites or farmers' fields," Pete continued. "In the case of the former, you have campgrounds that can accommodate hundreds of tents, with hookups for RVs and a host of other amenities; in the latter, you can knock on a farmer's door, pay a pittance, and have a spot to pitch your tent, nothing more."

Pete shared a few favorite camping spots around the park that provide exposure to its many appeals. "In the eastern section of the park, I like a spot called Side Farm, near the village of Patterdale. It's at the southern end of Ullswater, the second-largest lake in the district, and the valley is extremely picturesque. From here you have easy access to some of the tourist attractions in the region, like the Beatrix Potter museum (just over a pass in Ambleside), and the Ullswater Steamer leaves from a dock that's a walking distance away. A trail from the campground leads up to Striding Edge, what many consider to be the finest footpath in the Lake District—though it's a challenging hike, you're almost rock climbing at times. Another great hike that's better suited for less adventurous walkers also leaves right from Side Farm. You walk to the village of Glenridding and get on the steamer to Howtown. You get off the boat in Howtown and walk back along the shore. There's some up and down, but not more than a few hundred feet at a time. The trail takes you through the woods, past waterfalls, and out again to the shore, where you're confronted with expansive views of the mountains and lake, each time a bit different. At some points you're high above the lake, at others you're right along the shore. There's a shingle beach where you can swim if the weather is good. The trail leads right back to the campground. [Many believe that the site that inspired "Daffodils" is near Patterdale by Ullswater.]

"Another fine spot to camp is at Langdale, which is at the heart of the district. There are no lakes nearby, but you're surrounded by wonderful hills and walks galore. One short walk takes you up to Stickle Tarn, below the imposing cliffs of Pavey Ark, which can be great for swimming. [The lovely village of Elterwater, with its quintessential Lakeland pub, the Britannia Inn, is here as well.] A third option is Wasdale, which is in the west Lake District. It's different in atmosphere from the central and eastern districts, as it's quite remote. To reach Wasdale, you have to drive outside of the park and all the way around . . . or take a roller-coaster ride on a very narrow and steep single track road across the passes of Wrynose and Hardknott. If you make the effort to get here, the reward is a camping spot with an amazing view of the Scafell mountain range at the head of Wastwater. In fact, this view of Wasdale Head was adapted for the National Parks emblem. Wasdale is famed for having the Lake District's highest mountain, its deepest lake, and its smallest church. If you're coming to the Lake District for the first time and have limited time, I'd advise you to visit the east or central regions; Wasdale would make a great base for a second visit."

If you enjoy hiking and make it to the Lake District, you may wish to conquer Scafell Pike, which happens to be convenient to Wasdale. "You can climb Scafell from four different valleys, each with its own unique character and scenery. I like to approach from the north, via the hamlet of Seathwaite. You first ascend Glaramara [2,560 feet]; if the weather is clear, you'll have a three-hundred-and-sixty-degree panorama of the other peaks of the Lake District. Next, you'll cross a grassy ridge that connects to Allen Crags, then to Esk Hause. The hause (a Cumbrian word for "pass") which was once a key route for trade between the valleys of Eskdale and Borrowdale, brings you to the flanks of Ill Crag and boulder-strewn Broad Crag. After a bit of scrambling, you'll walk the last three hundred feet to Scafell Pike [3,210 feet] itself, where you can look south to Wales and west to the sea and Ireland.

"Sometimes when you're walking along a ridge, you might experience a cloud inversion. You might even be walking in the clouds. Suddenly it will clear and you'll see ridge after ridge like islands in a sea of clouds. If it happens to be near sunset and the clouds disperse, you may see the twinkling lights of a village below, where a pint of beer awaits."

PETE ROYALL was born and raised on Walney Island in the "South Lakeland." By the age of fourteen he was spending most of his weekends exploring the mountains and valleys of the Lake District National Park. By the age of sixteen he had discovered the joys of granite, and his exploration grew to encompass climbing the crags and cliffs of the mountain faces. Several seasons of climbing in the highlands of Scotland and the European Alps led to exploration in the Himalayas and eventually most of the World's Greater Ranges. Since 1992, Pete has led treks and expeditions to the Nepal and Indian Himalayas, the Karakoram and Hindu Kush ranges of Pakistan and Afghanistan, and the South American Andes. During this time, he has taken close to a hundred groups into the World's Greater Ranges for Britain's premier real-adventure travel company, KE Adventure Travel, and has pioneered new routes in the Himalayas and the Karakoram mountains, including first pass crossings and first ascents of unclimbed peaks. Pete also leads trips around Great Britain through his company, Wandering Aengus Treks (www.wandering-aengustreks.com).

If You Go

▶ **Getting There:** The Lake District is roughly one and a half hours north of Manchester, England, which is served by most major international carriers. There is also train service from London.

▶ **Best Time to Visit:** You'll find the mildest weather in the summer months, though you'll also find the largest crowds.

▶ **Campgrounds:** Pete Royall recommends three campgrounds: in the east district, Side Farm (+44 17684 82337); in the central district, Great Langdale (which offers full services, including yurt-like pods); and in the west district, Wasdale (which also offers pods). You can reserve spots at Great Langdale and Wasdale by visiting the National Trust website (www.nationaltrust.org.uk).

▶ **Activities:** Hiking, biking, rock climbing, sailing, canoeing, swimming, and fishing.

DRY TORTUGAS NATIONAL PARK

RECOMMENDED BY **Linda Friar**

If the thought of pitching a tent on a secluded beach—*a very secluded beach*—has appeal, you might consider hopping a ferry to one of America's most remote national parks: Dry Tortugas.

"As far as locations go, there's nothing else like it," Linda Friar began. "The park is seventy-plus miles off the coast of Key West. There's spectacular snorkeling, swimming, and fishing all against the backdrop of a historic nineteenth-century fort. It takes some planning to make for a good camping experience, as you have to take everything in and take everything out. But you'll have trouble finding a similar experience so removed from any development."

The Dry Tortugas are a group of seven small islands due west of Key West; the largest, Loggerhead Key, is less than 650 acres in size. (The other Keys include Garden, Bush, Long, Hospital, Middle, and East.) The first European to land here was Ponce de León, who harvested a number of sea turtles from around the islands, giving the keys their name. For a time, the Tortugas made a fine base for pirates marauding merchant ships in the Gulf of Mexico, but the absence of fresh water discouraged any permanent settlers. Campers have the War of 1812 (at least in part) to thank for Dry Tortugas National Park. After the war, there was a movement among American leaders to construct a series of forts along the coast. The Dry Tortugas were identified as an ideal site for a garrison to protect and provision ships plying the Straits of Florida and the Gulf of Mexico, and in 1846 work began at Garden Key on what would become Fort Jefferson. (A lighthouse had been built on Garden Key twenty years earlier, as the reefs in the region posed great danger to shipping traffic.) The fort—an imposing six-sided structure—was never completed. Still, with some sixteen million red bricks used in its unfinished construction, it

remains the largest all-masonry fort in the United States. For a time, the fort was used to house prisoners—many of whom were Union Army deserters. After its stint as a prison, Garden Key was used to store coal to fuel naval ships. A strong hurricane destroyed the coal works. By 1908, Garden Key and the other Tortugas had been designated a bird reserve, by 1935 a national monument, and by 1992 a national park.

To reach Dry Tortugas National Park you must first make your way to Key West, and then board the *Yankee Freedom III* ferry; the engine-powered catamaran runs every day and takes roughly two hours to reach Garden Key. While the passage can be a bit rough, depending on weather conditions, the *Yankee Freedom III* utilizes a state-of-the-art ride control system to soften the passage. Upon arrival, some campers will opt to wheel their gear to the ten-site camping area (in carts provided) and join the forty-minute tour provided by the ferry operators. "Highlights include a chance to visit the area of the fort where Dr. Samuel Mudd [an alleged conspirator in the assassination of Abraham Lincoln] was held prisoner," said Nick Fueschel, a National Park Service ranger who's worked at Dry Tortugas. "People also enjoy seeing the cannons on top of the fort—fifteen-inch smooth-bore Rodmans." [These cannons—the cutting edge of artillery circa 1865—weigh twenty-five tons apiece and could fire a 432-pound projectile three miles. It took seven soldiers to operate a fifteen-inch Rodman.]

Fort Jefferson is certainly an attraction for Dry Tortugas visitors, but the turquoise waters and powdery white sand are an even greater draw. There are four beaches (South Swim, North Swim, Seaplane, and Dinghy) to explore and a number of fine snorkeling spots. One of the best snorkeling areas is near the ruins of the North Coaling Dock. Though the storage structures here were destroyed, the pilings remain. The shelter the pilings provide and their proximity to a deep channel make this area a great spot to encounter some of the park's larger marine animals, including tarpon, goliath groupers, barracuda, and sharks. An assemblage of hard and soft corals, numerous reef fish (including parrot fish and sergeant majors), and vast schools of silversides are present. Though nearly hunted to extinction, five species of sea turtles—loggerhead, green, leatherback, Kemp's ridley, and hawksbill—are still present in the waters around the park. Another reptile—the American crocodile—is occasionally encountered in the waters off the Dry Tortugas. Though fearsome in appearance, American crocs are far less aggressive than their man-eating Australian cousins . . . but you'll do well to keep a healthy distance. "My favorite snorkeling encounter at the park came when I found myself swimming inside a

OPPOSITE: Fort Jefferson dominates Garden Key, and is the largest all-masonry fort in the United States . . . though it was never completed.

18

DESTINATION

bait ball of silversides," ranger Nick shared. "Suddenly the silversides were being corralled by six-foot-long tarpon from the outside."

The Dry Tortugas are also a magnet for birding enthusiasts. Almost three hundred species have been identified around the islands, including a host of pelagic (open ocean) birds like frigatebirds. You're almost sure to find sooty terns—some 100,000 nest on Bush Key, which is adjacent to Garden Key.

As Linda alludes to above, a camping trip to the Dry Tortugas takes a good deal of planning. You need to bring everything—water, charcoal, or Sterno for cooking (no gas or propane allowed) and any other camping gear you might need. Of course, you need to pack everything out. But, for your $3-per-person fee, you get a picnic table, a grill, and a bit of shade from waving palm trees. "It's certainly a rustic experience," Linda added. "But you won't soon forget the open vistas, the quiet once the day visitors have left, the sunsets, and the vibrancy of the starry night skies."

LINDA FRIAR is chief of public affairs at Everglades and Dry Tortugas National Parks. She is also an adjunct professor at Florida Atlantic University and serves as lead information officer for the National Park Service Eastern All Risk Incident Management Team. She is a graduate of Florida Atlantic University.

If You Go

▶ **Getting There:** The Dry Tortugas are reached via the *Yankee Freedom* ferry (800-634-0939; www.drytortugas.com) from Key West. The seventy-mile ride takes two hours.

▶ **Best Time to Visit:** The park is open year-round. January through May will see the lowest temperatures and humidity.

▶ **Campgrounds:** A ten-site, primitive campground is located on Garden Key (the same island as Fort Jefferson). Campers must bring *everything* they need, including water. Picnic tables, grills, and a composting toilet are provided. Sites are first come, first served, and cost $3 per person.

▶ **Activities:** Snorkeling, fishing, stargazing, sightseeing.

THE GERS

RECOMMENDED BY **Rod Wheat**

The region of the Gers in the southwest corner of France is a far cry from the fast pace of Paris or the glitz and glamour of the Côte d'Azur. But for those seeking a bucolic retreat, its pastoral setting will not disappoint.

"We love to send clients to Le Camp de Florence in the Gers region," began Rod Wheat. "It provides a stunning setting, adjacent to an ancient fortified village. There's a sleepy ambiance to the place. You feel almost like you're in another time, nestled among the rolling fields of sunflowers, in the shadow of the Collegiate Church in La Romieu."

The Gers, part of the Gascony region in the Midi-Pyrénées, is considered one of western Europe's most rural regions, a land still largely given over to agrarian endeavors. (It takes its name from the Gers river, a tributary of the larger Garonne.) Known to many as the stomping grounds of the Three Musketeers (brought to life by author Alexandre Dumas and based upon a *gersois* man named d'Artagnan), the region has also been home to much real swordplay. The Vandals and Visigoths ravaged the area during the Dark Ages. In the Middle Ages, the Hundred Years' War with the English (from 1337 to 1453) was fought in the region over possession of Aquitaine; later battles were fought in the 1500s and 1600s between Catholics and Protestant Huguenots over the primacy of their faiths. The centuries of unrest led to the prominence of bastides (fortified villages) in the Gers; to this day, nearly one-third of *gersois* villages are medieval bastides.

Le Camp de Florence spreads over twenty-five acres, allowing ample space and a sense of privacy for each campsite. There are a host of "camping" options for visitors, ranging from one-, two-, and three-bedroom trailers (with all the comforts of home); to yurt-style lodging; to sites for tents or recreational vehicles. As is common in Europe, Le Camp de

Florence is more full-service family resort than bare-bones campground. There is an outdoor pool replete with a waterslide; a toddler's pool, trampoline, playground, and bouncy house for younger visitors; tennis courts, several restaurants, a bar and disco for older visitors; and Wi-Fi connectivity throughout. (Indeed, mom and dad can relax in the shade of century-old chestnut trees, sipping a drink in the bar area while the kids enjoy the pool a few yards away.) You can also arrange to have fresh bread delivered to your domicile each morning—a touch of French cultivation, to be sure.

One of the appeals of Le Camp de Florence—especially for visitors curious about French history—is its proximity to La Romieu. The village was established in the eleventh century by pilgrims who were making their way to Santiago de Compostela in the Spanish autonomous region of Galicia, where tradition has it that the bones of St. James (believed to be one of the twelve apostles of Jesus) are buried. In the center of the village is the Collegiate Church of St. Peter, which was built in the fourteenth century and is now recognized as a UNESCO World Heritage site for its excellent representation of southern European Gothic architecture. The church—including a sacristy decorated with polychromatic frescoes that date back to the structure's inception—can be toured. There are fantastic panoramic views of the surrounding countryside from one of the church's octagonal towers. Visitors will notice whimsical feline sculptures around the village. These pay tribute to the legend of a girl named Angéline and her cats, which (as the story goes) helped rid the village of rats and thus stave off famine. Another attraction is the Gardens of Coursiana, an arboretum that showcases seven hundred species of trees and plants from around the world.

Though the more arduous trails of the MidiPyrénées lie to the south, the gently rolling terrain of the Gers is very popular with walkers. Many trails depart from the campground. Some connect to El Camino de Santiago, which was the route for one of the most important pilgrimages in medieval times and was walked by millions of the faithful. (There are actually five routes for the Way of St. James; the route that passes through La Romieu is known as the French Way and has been the most popular since the eleventh century.) Walking the trails around La Romieu, one may still come upon pilgrims, many of whom have a scallop shell on their backpack, a longstanding symbol of El Camino de Santiago. (Signs and buildings along the trail to Santiago de Compostela also sported the scallop shell.) Le Camp de Florence remains a popular stopover spot for modern pilgrims. (Biking on these same trails and quiet area roads is also popular.)

Almost every region in France has its noteworthy contributions to the universe of gastronomy, and Gascony is no different. Indeed, the region has been gaining a great deal of attention as one of France's recently discovered foodie hot spots. Wonderfully rich soil and a warm climate foster abundant fruit orchards that yield plums, peaches, nectarines, kiwis, and apples, as well as a wide variety of vegetables. A number of grape varietals are grown for wine making, including Ugni Blanc. These grapes also find their way into what may be the region's most celebrated drink, Armagnac, a distinctive brandy. Gascony's best-known culinary contributions are decidedly earthy and will induce vegetarians (and cardiologists) to cringe. These include confit (duck legs poached in duck fat and stored in duck lard for months or years), blood sausage, *magret* (duck breast), charcuterie (using all parts of the pig), and foie gras made from both duck and geese. Most of these specialties can be found at public markets and restaurants in the towns of the Gers. If you don't wish to wander far from your pitch, the restaurant at Le Camp de Florence receives high marks.

ROD WHEAT is campsites director for Alan Rogers, which organizes and books camping and caravanning holidays throughout Europe. The company represents more than five thousand locations.

If You Go

▶ **Getting There:** Visitors can fly into Pau, which is served via Paris by Air France (+33 892 702 654; www.airfrance.fr). It's roughly a ninety-minute drive from the airport to Le Camp de Florence.

▶ **Best Time to Visit:** The camping season in the Gers runs from April to mid-October.

▶ **Campgrounds:** Le Camp de Florence (+33 562 28 1558; www.lecampdeflorence.com) comes highly recommended. Tent sites during the high season begin at €36 for two adults per night. Booking is available through Alan Rogers (+44 1580 214 000; www.alanrogers.com).

▶ **Activities:** Swimming, hiking, biking, and cultural sightseeing.

WALDSEILGARTEN HÖLLSCHLUCHT

RECOMMENDED BY **Markus Depprich**

There's a certain exhilaration that comes with high-elevation camping. The crisp mountain air and sense of being a bit closer to the sky are invigorating, a balm to the senses. Visitors to Waldseilgarten Höllschlucht have the opportunity to take camping to a new, higher level . . . literally. Here, campers eschew the geographic limitations of campgrounds, opting instead to pitch their "tent" among the infinitely airy possibilities of the atmosphere.

Waldseilgarten Höllschlucht rests near the village of Pfronten, in the southern section of the German state of Bavaria, southwest of Munich. The region, known as the Allgäu, rests in the shadow of the Bavarian Alps, and is celebrated for its bucolic scenery. "We have hills and mountains, but not too high, up to 6,500 feet," Markus described. "In the early summer, farmers bring their cows up to the mountain meadows of the Alps to feed; they come back down in the early fall. [The traditional descent of the cows from the mountains around the Allgäu—known as the *Viehscheid*—happens throughout September and is marked by many traditional celebrations, complete with Bavarian beer and music.] People do mountain touring in summer and winter, sometimes staying overnight in huts. There are more than ten lakes within less than fifteen miles of Waldseilgarten Höllschlucht; many of these have campgrounds." Though none of these campgrounds let you zip up your sleeping bag in the air!

Waldseilgarten Höllschlucht's "air tents" utilize portaledges, which (as its name strongly implies) is a portable ledge that was initially designed to allow rock climbers to set up a bed or shelter as they tackled a multiday pitch. Some trace the birth of portaledges to the climbers at Yosemite National Park, who liberated cots from camps in the valley in the sixties and outfitted them with straps (presumably quite strong) that required only a single anchor point. Before the creation of these early portaledges, climbers relied

OPPOSITE:

*A portaledge
enables visitors
at Waldseilgarten
Höllschlucht
to take their tent
camping to a
new level . . .
literally.*

20

DESTINATION

95

on hammocks, which required two anchor points . . . and since they were affixed to the rock wall in question, would become soaked if it happened to rain and were uncomfortable (at best) for sleeping. By the 1980s, several portaledges had been developed for the marketplace. Today's portaledge still needs only one anchor point and is supported by four- or six-point suspensions; it resembles a hanging tent.

At Waldseilgarten Höllschlucht, there are three options for aerial camping. The first takes place on the grounds of the resort's High Ropes Course, where a platform is suspended from trees roughly twenty-five feet above the ground. Campers use ropes to climb up to the platform and can descend when necessary to answer nature's call at nearby restrooms; a nearby waterfall provides a most invigorating morning shower. Option two takes you into the forest, where you'll take your rest in a portaledge tent hanging from a sturdy tree branch. This is Waldseilgarten Höllschlucht's most popular air-camping experience. Markus described how the day unfolds.

"Guests usually arrive around lunchtime. That gives them time to explore the High Ropes Course and to warm up in general. The course has a number of different levels of varying difficulty, so people unaccustomed to climbing can get used to it slowly. For climbing up to the tent, we use a device called an ascender (which attaches to a rope to facilitate climbing), and you have a chance to practice using it with a guide. Using the ascender requires some strength, though people of average physical ability can certainly do it. Before leaving for the camping spot, we'll either cook dinner over a barbecue or visit a traditional Bavarian restaurant. Then we pack up the portaledge, your sleeping bags, and clothing and head into the woods. Your guide will work with you to hang the tent in the trees. Then you'll climb up—anywhere from ten to twenty feet—hopefully in time to enjoy the sunset. (It's a good idea to do your toilet before you reach your tent!) Though the portaledge is safe, it's not completely stable; you'll sway a bit, especially if there's any wind. But you're firmly belayed, so you needn't worry if you turn in your sleep. Your guide stays fairly nearby in case you need any help or wish to come down, but not so close as to impede on your privacy. You have a feeling of being very close to nature." When you wake up the next morning, you climb down, pack up the tent/portaledge and head back to the High Ropes Course for breakfast. Campers have the option of sticking around to do more climbing on the ropes course, or to take advantage of Waldseilgarten Höllschlucht's archery range.

If you enjoy bivouacking from a tree and have a taste for adventure, the guides at Waldseilgarten Höllschlucht can help you experience a bit of big wall camping with

DESTINATION 20

option three, Bavarian style. Your guide will rappel with a tent, and then you'll make your way down the cliff face to your portaledge—up to one thousand feet above the valley floor—for a most unique night's sleep. (As you might expect, this option is not recommended for acrophobes.)

Once you've returned to terra firma, consider exploring some of the Allgäu's more earthbound attractions. "Many people tour Neuschwanstein Castle," Markus explained. "This is the most famous of the castles that King Ludwig II commissioned and is said to have inspired the castle in the Disney logo." Tours highlight the influence the operas of Richard Wagner had on Neuschwanstein's construction, including its finely detailed murals. You'll also want a chance to savor some of Bavaria's hearty cuisine. "There are tasty cheeses, like the Allgäuer Bergkäse mountain cheese," Markus added. "People also associate Bavaria with Weisswurst, or 'white sausage,' which is famous throughout Bavaria. [Legend says it was invented by accident in Munich.] A dish that's very traditional in the Allgäu is Allgäuer Kässpätzle, which combines spätzle, cheeses, and onions. Of course, Kässpätzle is best when washed down with a mug of beer brewed by a local brewery like Kössel Bräu or Zötler."

MARKUS DEPPRICH has lived in Bavaria for all of his life and works as a freelance trainer for outdoor education and team building in the summer and a ski instructor in the winter. His passions include skiing, hiking, and mountain climbing. He is currently a guide at Waldseilgarten Höllschlucht. His travels have taken him to New Zealand, Australia, and Nepal.

If You Go

▶ **Getting There:** Waldseilgarten is roughly two hours southwest of Munich, which is served by most major carriers.
▶ **Best Time to Visit:** Portaledge camping is available May through September.
▶ **Campgrounds:** Waldseilgarten (+49 83 63 9 25 98 96; www.waldseilgarten-hoellschlucht.de) offers portaledge camping by previous arrangement. Tree camping begins at €250 per person. While platform camping can be enjoyed by families with younger children, portaledge camping is reserved for campers sixteen years or older.
▶ **Activities:** Rope climbing, hiking, archery, sightseeing.

REDFISH LAKE

RECOMMENDED BY **Terry Clark**

A pristine alpine lake backed by soaring mountains. A sprawling wilderness area where the same ecosystems and animals that thrived here before Lewis and Clark's expedition remain extant. A homey, family-style resort that harkens back to summer vacations of a bygone era.

All of these elements come together at Redfish Lake in central Idaho.

"The region around Stanley, Idaho, is well known as an outdoor recreation hub," Terry Clark began, "and Redfish Lake is the focus of outdoor recreation in greater Stanley. You're surrounded by the Sawtooth National Recreation Area, more than 750,000 acres of mostly undeveloped country. The lake itself is five miles long and very clear, with the Sawtooth Mountains rising abruptly to the west, including Grand Mogul [elevation 9,733 feet] and Mount Heyburn [elevation 10,239 feet]. On the northern end of the lake, there's a quaint lodge, a small marina, a boat ramp, and a little store. The rest of the lakeshore (and beyond) is undeveloped. You can take a boat shuttle from the north side of the lake to the south side for twelve dollars. Walk five minutes or so, and you're in the Sawtooth Wilderness."

Redfish Lake takes its name from the vast numbers of sockeye salmon that once migrated here from the Pacific, a voyage of some nine hundred miles (the longest migration of any salmon species). Dams on the Columbia and Snake River systems nearly drove Redfish Lake sockeye to extinction; some might recall "Lonesome Larry," the single salmon that returned to the lake in 1991. Larry's story galvanized government efforts to resuscitate the run, and thanks to the Redfish Lake Sockeye Captive Broodstock Program, more than 1,500 fish returned to the lake in 2013. "I wouldn't say that the sockeye runs have recovered," Terry continued, "but they are certainly making progress." Fishing is an attraction for many visitors to Redfish Lake, though the sockeye are not the target. Instead,

OPPOSITE:
A stand up paddleboarder takes in the Sawtooths from beautiful Redfish Lake.

LAKE GARDA

RECOMMENDED BY **Russell Wheldon**

Lake Garda sits in northern Italy, just west of the town of Verona, which was popularized by Shakespeare's *Two Gentlemen of Verona*. It's Italy's largest lake, stretching over thirty miles in length and reaching a maximum width of ten miles and a depth of more than one thousand feet. In the north, the lake is encircled by mountains, the southern reach of the Italian Alps; in the south, by hills scoured by receding glaciers. Garda's waters are exceptionally clear and pleasantly cool, and have attracted holiday seekers from the north and south for many generations; in fact, 7 percent of all tourists to Italy visit Lake Garda.

There are a number of camping options around Lake Garda. Russell Wheldon prefers Fornella Camping for clients who are seeking an Italian lake experience. "Fornella is one of the few campsites on Lake Garda still surrounded by olive plantations," he offered. "It's still retained a true country atmosphere. Many sites look out over the lake. Those that don't have fine views of the surrounding hills and the orchards. The lake is of course a main attraction, and Fornella has excellent facilities for water-sports enthusiasts, whether you're a boater or a windsurfer."

There are a host of different accommodation options at Fornella. Simple cabins (with all the amenities of home) are available in two- and three-bedroom configurations, both on the lake and set back in the olive orchards. "Safari tents" (which resemble yurts) also provide a more glamping-oriented experience. There are also more than 250 sites for tents or recreational vehicles. All come equipped with electricity, and many have water as well. As is the case in many campgrounds in Europe, Wi-Fi is available throughout Fornella. If you don't feel like cooking, there's both a full-service restaurant and a pizzeria. If you do, there's a store on premises to secure provisions. There are a number of pool options available around the campground and two beaches—the "morning beach" (which

OPPOSITE:
Isola del Garda
was once visited
by St. Francis of
Assisi, and is a
short boat ride
from Fornella
Camping.

DESTINATION 22

faces the southeast) and the "evening beach" (which faces the southwest and has the advantage of proximity to the bar). The beaches are composed of smallish pebbles, so consider water shoes if your feet are sensitive.

Many visitors to Lake Garda will take to the water. Constant winds make the lake an attractive sailing venue, with the *Pelér* blowing reliably from north to south in the morning and the *Ora* coming up in the afternoon and blowing south to north. Many regattas are held here, and Fornella Camping has a marina where guests can moor boats that are brought to the lake. Windsurfing—and increasingly, kiteboarding—are also popular, especially on the northern side of the lake. (Many concessionaires rent boards and provide lessons for those new to the sport.) The marina at Fornella also has small motorboats available for rent for those less interested in plying the winds.

Whether you sail, windsurf, or take an excursion boat, you'll want to voyage to Isola del Garda, an island in the southwestern section of Lake Garda (not far from Fornella Camping) that's rich in both beauty and history. St. Francis of Assisi visited the island around 1220. Recognizing its isolation from the hubbub of daily life, he established a simple hermitage here for his monks. The island stayed in church hands for the next five hundred years and eventually came into private ownership. In the 1890s, the villa that marks the island today was constructed in lavish neo-Gothic–Venetian style. Isola del Garda was initially barren, but its inhabitants conveyed soil to its shores, slowly transforming the rocky landscape to a lushly forested setting that includes formal gardens and a park. Today, the island is owned by the Borghese Cavazza family (who owns Fornella Camping), and guided tours (in English, Italian, and German) are offered from April through October. One stylish option for touring Isola Del Garda is via *Siora Veronica*, a two-masted gaff schooner that once served as a barge for Lake Garda residents before roads were constructed along the lake's perimeter. Concerts are also offered on the island throughout the summer.

Italy is a land of gastronomic delights, and the Lake Garda region is no different. Olives are one of the most important crops in the area and are pressed to make extra-virgin olive oil. The Borghese Cavazza family has been olive farming here since the late 1800s. (Oil pressed in this region is celebrated for its delicacy and lightness.) Lake Garda is also known for its lemons, which were introduced in the thirteenth century from the Middle East and now find their way into a number of local recipes, which include lemon cream, a popular soft drink, and Limoncino liqueur. (Lake Garda's citrus crop inspired the region's "lemon houses," large structures with removable roofs that were built to shelter the delicate lemon trees during the winter months. Several lemon houses have been restored and may now be toured.) At the dinner table, you may encounter *salada*, a salted beef that's often served raw and tortellini, delicate handmade pasta rings filled with meat or cheese and served with melted butter, sage, and Parmesan or in soup. Fish harvested from the lake—whitefish, pike, perch, and trout—also make their way onto the menu. Grana Padano is a favorite cheese produced in the region. Any Lake Garda meal can be enhanced with one of the fine wines produced in the area, which include Nosiola, Cabernet, Vino Santo, and Classico Groppello della Valtenesi. Grappa is a favorite aperitif, sometimes flavored with herbs, berries, juniper, and dried roots.

RUSSELL WHELDON is commercial director for Alan Rogers, which organizes and books camping and caravanning holidays throughout Europe. The company represents more than five thousand locations.

If You Go

▶ **Getting There:** Visitors can fly into Verona, which has service from many European cities on a number of different airlines. It's roughly an hour's drive from the airport to Fornella Camping.

▶ **Best Time to Visit:** The camping season around Lake Garda runs from mid-April to mid-October. Summertime can be hot, but the lake remains refreshingly cool.

▶ **Campgrounds:** Fornella Camping (+39 0365 62294; www.fornellacamping.com) comes highly recommended. Tent sites during the high season begin at €13.50 per adult, €8.70 per child. Booking is available through Alan Rogers (+44 1580 214 000; www.alan-rogers.com).

▶ **Activities:** Swimming, boating, fishing, biking, hiking, and cultural sightseeing.

MAMMOTH CAVE NATIONAL PARK

RECOMMENDED BY **Vickie Carson**

"The beauty of Mammoth Cave is that it's two parks in one," began Vickie Carson. "First, there's the underground park. Mammoth is the longest known cave system in the world, with over four hundred miles of subterranean habitat that have been explored. The cave has wonderful historical, geological, and biological assets. The other park at Mammoth is aboveground. The surface world here is really closely connected to the underground world. The rugged karst topography illustrates how water drains and creates rock formations. There are two beautiful rivers flowing through the park, the Green and Nolin. They provide kayaking, canoeing, and fishing opportunities. There are also miles and miles of trails that lead people into the backcountry. It's hard to find solitude in today's world. At Mammoth, you can find such solitude in a cave, on the river, or in the woods."

Mammoth Cave National Park encompasses more than fifty thousand acres in central Kentucky. Human presence in the cave (technically known as the Mammoth–Flint Ridge Cave System) dates back more than five thousand years, though its discovery by Europeans did not occur until the 1790s (one story goes that a hunter came upon an entrance while chasing a wounded bear). Soon after, saltpeter—a key component of gunpowder—was discovered in the cave and mined. By the 1830s, the cave's value as a tourist attraction was beginning to be exploited. (The very first cave tour was offered in 1816.) A slave named Stephen Bishop discovered many of the passages that are shared today. By the 1880s, a railroad line had been established to bring visitors to Mammoth. By the 1920s, acrimony between competing tour operators led to the so-called Kentucky Cave War. "I first visited Mammoth as a child, and then later on a trip with my Girl Scout troop," Vickie recalled. "The park is near Interstate 65, and many people first come upon it as they travel north

OPPOSITE:
Tours of
Mammoth
Cave are an
essential part of
the Mammoth
Cave National
Park experience.

23

DESTINATION

or south on longer trips. Seeing the cave is a memorable experience that brings people back . . . often with their kids or grandkids."

Most who visit Mammoth Cave National Park wish to experience its subterranean wonders. "There's really something for everyone in terms of interests and activity level," Vickie continued. "The Frozen Niagara Tour is well suited for people who have trouble walking or families with young children. It's almost all flat, goes only a quarter mile and takes less than one hour and a half. It gives you a great taste of the cave's complexity, including the Frozen Niagara formation. At the other end of the spectrum, there's the Wild Cave Tour, a five-mile, six-hour expedition where you crawl, climb, stoop, belly crawl through dry, dusty areas, water, and mud. People come out so dirty, but they're proud of their dirt. There's also the Trog Tour, a kids-only expedition where everyone gets a hard hat, coveralls, and a headlamp and travels along routes off the main trail. My personal favorite is the Historic Tour. This takes you through the parts of the cave that have been toured the longest. You'll hit all the famous landmarks—Bottomless Pit, Fat Man's Misery, and Mammoth Dome, the gymnasium-size chambers that gave Mammoth its name. Whichever tour you take, there's usually a moment when the tour leader turns off the lights. Suddenly there's no natural light, and little sound. It's a multisensory experience. The darkness and quiet leave a long-lasting impression on visitors. The cave is an alien world, like nothing on the earth's surface. Down below, you lose sense of time and direction. It grabs your imagination."

The fun at Mammoth Cave National Park doesn't end when you return to the light. While conditions may be quite a bit warmer and more humid when you leave the cave, you'll find many ways to cool off. "Some trails lead to cave springs that run out of the side of hills," Vickie said. "The water's a pleasingly cool fifty-four degrees; these little streams are emptying water out of the cave and into the Green River. It is a great river to play in; there are islands, gravel bars, riffles, pools, but no scary rapids. It's good for people of all ages. There are several liveries where you can rent a canoe or kayak." The park also has trails for horseback riding and mountain biking, and many road-biking opportunities.

There are two campgrounds at Mammoth for individual parties and one group site. Vickie described the options: "Mammoth Cave is the biggest campground with one hundred and nine sites. Though it's close to the visitor center and there's a store and showers nearby, it's very serene in the evening. We're not that far from populated areas, but the hardwood forest blocks the horizon, so the star viewing can be impressive. There's quite a din at night between the frogs, bugs, and birds. If you pass by in the morning, the smell of campfire and bacon will pull you in. Houchin Ferry is the other campground for individuals. It's much smaller—just twelve sites—and is a little more secluded. Houchin Ferry is right on the Green River, so fishermen can cast right from the bank for bluegill, catfish, bass, perch, and crappie. There are also twelve backcountry campsites north of the Green River and a group/equestrian campground at Maple Springs. The campgrounds in the park are fairly primitive in terms of amenities. Private campgrounds outside the park offer more services."

Mammoth Cave National Park is open to camping from March through November, and each season has something different to offer. "In the spring, the wildflowers are in bloom," Vickie continued, "and they are easy to see before the green foliage comes off. In the summer, the woods are dense and junglelike. In the fall, the foliage is beautiful—oak, gum, dogwood, tulip, poplars, and sassafras, all in brilliant colors."

VICKIE CARSON is a public information officer for Mammoth Cave National Park. She has worked for the National Park Service for thirty-six years, most of her career at Mammoth. Vickie considers herself a grown-up Girl Scout.

If You Go

▶ **Getting There:** Mammoth Cave National Park is equidistant from Louisville, Kentucky, and Nashville, Tennessee (roughly ninety miles), both of which are served by many carriers.

▶ **Best Time to Visit:** The park is open March through November. Summers are busiest, though spring and fall have cooler temperatures. Most cave tours are offered throughout the year.

▶ **Campgrounds:** Of the three campgrounds at Mammoth—Mammoth Cave, Houchin Ferry, and Maple Springs Group Campground—Mammoth Cave offers the most amenities. Site fees range from $12 to $20.

▶ **Activities:** Cave tours, hiking, canoeing/kayaking, mountain biking, and fishing.

BAXTER STATE PARK

RECOMMENDED BY **Greg Blanchette**

"I grew up in southern Maine, and my father was an enthusiastic hiker and camper," Greg Blanchette recalled. "When I was seven or eight, he took me on my first camping trip to Baxter State Park. I mostly remember it being a very long ways away, one dirt road after another. My dad died when I was nine, and it took some time before I made it north to the park again. When I was twenty-one, I went up to climb Mount Katahdin—a rite of passage for a Maine kid. A few years later I began going up more frequently, both in the summer to hike and fish and in the winter to cross-country ski."

Baxter State Park occupies a 209,501-acre swath of north central Maine. Once the domain of the Wabanaki Native American tribe, moose, and the Great Northern Paper Company, the region's mountains, lakes, and possibilities for nature-loving first came to the attention of Percival Baxter in 1903 during a fishing trip. Baxter, a scion of a wealthy Portland family, was taken with the area's beauty and utter wildness, and as his political influence waxed, so did his efforts to have the area preserved as a park.

As governor, he was unable to sway the legislature, but Baxter would not be deterred. His opportunity came with the crash of 1929. In 1930, cash-poor Great Northern Paper Company agreed to sell Baxter the 6,000 acres of land that included Mount Katahdin for $25,000. Baxter in turn deeded this land to the state of Maine, with the proviso that the land "shall forever be used for public park and recreational purposes, shall be forever left in the natural wild state, shall forever be kept as a sanctuary for wild beasts and birds, that no road or ways for motor vehicles shall hereafter ever be constructed thereon or therein." Over the remainder of his life, Percival Baxter purchased nearly 200,000 more acres of land west and north of his original acquisition, deeding it to the state. Upon his death in 1969, he bequeathed $7 million for the park's ongoing maintenance.

OPPOSITE:
Mount Katahdin looms over Daicey Pond in Baxter State Park.

DESTINATION **24**

111

Baxter's assertion that Katahdin would one day be viewed as the state of Maine's crowning glory received a most powerful endorsement a few years back when L.L.Bean adopted the mountain as part of its logo.

Baxter boasts eight front-country campgrounds and a number of backcountry sites. Greg has sampled both. "When my children were younger, we'd often head to South Branch Pond Campground," he continued. "It's at the northern end of the park, away from Mount Katahdin and its many day-trippers, so it's pretty quiet. It's a great spot for kids. The campground rests on two ponds. There's a beach where kids can go swimming. Canoes are also available for rent (for a dollar an hour!), and the ponds are small enough that kids can paddle across and have an adventure without being too far away. There's also fishing for brook trout. A number of trails depart from the campground, and some are flat enough for easy family hikes; on one trail, along Howe Brook, there's a spot where you can ride down a natural rock slide on the brook. One of my favorite backcountry sites is Russell Pond. It used to be a logging camp; on the way in, you pass old cellar holes that used to be a school for loggers' children, and some contain discarded logging tools. You can almost envision the thriving logging camp that once occupied the area. It's about seven miles in, but not arduous at all; I think a ten-year-old could do it without much trouble, as you're going down an old logging road and there's no elevation gain. Though it doesn't take an expedition to get there, it feels very remote. The fishing on Russell Pond (and some of the other nearby ponds and streams) is very good, and there are canoes for rent. There are some tent sites at Russell as well as some lean-tos. There's also a bunkhouse that can accommodate eight people who don't want to bother with a tent. Each of the campgrounds in Baxter—even the backcountry sites—have a bunkhouse. This is really handy in the winter, as it allows you to cross-country ski across the park and have a warm place to stay."

There's abundant wildlife in Baxter State Park, including deer, black bear, and Maine's iconic ungulate, moose. Maine bull moose can reach weights up to 1,500 pounds and stand seven feet at the shoulder; populations are quite healthy in the park, and they can be encountered anytime and anywhere. If you don't come upon Mr. or Mrs. Moose on the trail, you have an excellent chance of finding Maine's totem mammal at Sandy Stream Pond near dusk.

There are nearly two hundred miles of trails in Baxter State Park and eighteen peaks that exceed three thousand feet. Like his father, Greg has encouraged his children to take an interest in hiking. He's found a willing taker in his daughter. "For the last four years, my daughter and I have hiked in different parts of Baxter," Greg shared. "A few years ago, we knew it was the last trip for a while, as she was heading off to school. We were hiking a route called the Classic Loop, which offers some incredible views of some of the park's iconic landmarks—Knife Edge, Baxter Peak (the highest point on Mount Katahdin), and the basins that surround Katahdin . . . the Northwest, North, and Great Basins. We hiked into Russell Pond, and then on to Davis Pond, which is the only spot in the park where you can see the Northwest Basin. When we woke up that morning, we were completely socked in by thick clouds. We resigned ourselves to missing these incredible views, and as we descended the Hamlin Ridge Trail, I began describing what we'd be seeing if it were clear—Knife Edge would be here, Baxter Peak there. Suddenly, the clouds lifted, and there were the Knife Edge and Baxter Peak. It was an incredible moment and the one I wanted her to experience. I have a photo of her looking up at the mountain on my desk."

GREG BLANCHETTE is inventory manager for L.L.Bean, Inc. An avid hiker and backpacker, he has completed Vermont's Long Trail and the Appalachian Trail in Maine, New Hampshire, and Vermont, and has climbed all the four-thousand-foot peaks of New England. Greg also enjoys fly-fishing.

If You Go

▶ **Getting There:** Baxter State Park is approximately 160 miles north of Portland, which is served by many carriers, including Delta (800-221-1212; www.delta.com) and United (800-864-8331; www.united.com).

▶ **Best Time to Visit:** The summer camping season is from May 15 to Oct. 15. The winter season runs from December through March. September is a wonderful time to visit.

▶ **Campgrounds:** There are eight campgrounds in Baxter State Park (www.baxterstateparkauthority.com). Campground lean-to or tent sites are $30 in the summer; bunkhouse beds begin at $11. Cabins are also available.

▶ **Activities:** Hiking, fishing, canoeing, cross-country skiing.

ACADIA NATIONAL PARK

RECOMMENDED BY **Charlie Jacobi**

Viewers of the ABC program *Good Morning America* named Acadia National Park "America's Favorite Place" in 2014. Charlie Jacobi isn't surprised.

"The first reason people want to come to Acadia is the stunning beauty of the place," he began. "That's one of the main reasons it was created: to preserve these landscapes. Almost everyone who comes to the park wants to head to the top of Cadillac Mountain to take in the views of the water and the islands . . . and at certain times of year, to be among the first people in the United States to see the sun. People also come to recreate. The park has a great assortment of hiking trails and carriage roads, which attract walkers and bicyclists. The park also has great sea kayaking and rock climbing. Maine has little publicly accessible shoreline; much of it resides in Acadia, and people come here to get close to the water. Finally, I think people are attracted to Acadia because of its accessibility. It's a small park, and it's possible to feel like you've absorbed much of it in a finite amount of time, unlike some of the big parks out west, like Yellowstone. There's an intimacy, and people readily become attached to it."

Most of Acadia National Park's granite headlands, rocky beaches, and spruce-fir forests are contained on Mount Desert Island, approximately three quarters of the way up Maine's sprawling coastline, and an hour or so's drive southeast from the city of Bangor. Acadia was the first national park established east of the Mississippi, and its 2.4 million annual visitors have the painters of the Hudson River School at least in part to thank. Frederic Church and Thomas Cole (among others) captured the region's beauty for city dwellers in the south, helping to draw the then-developing leisure class "down east" from Philadelphia, New York, and Boston. The affluent of the Gay Nineties (including Rockefellers, Vanderbilts, and Carnegies) built grand estates on the island, decamping

OPPOSITE: Isle Au Haut is a remote outpost of Acadia National Park that can only be reached by ferry.

DESTINATION

25

115

here for a portion of each summer. While the so-called robber barons changed the social face of Mount Desert Island, they were instrumental in setting aside the land that would eventually become a national park in 1919. Fearing the onslaught the surrounding woodlands would face with the development of a mobile, gasoline-powered sawmill, the summer citizenry were galvanized under the leadership of Charles Eliot and George B. Dorr, who spearheaded preservation efforts. Dorr would become the park's first superintendent. (John D. Rockefeller contributed another signature facet of the park—its forty-five miles of broken-stone carriage roads, now popular with bicyclists.)

There are several must-visit spots in Acadia. One is the summit of Cadillac Mountain, the tallest point along the eastern coast of the United States at 1,530 feet. You can drive to the summit on a winding road, though it may be more satisfying to reach the 360-degree views of Bar Harbor, Frenchman Bay, and the Cranberry Islands by reaching the top by foot on one of four trails—North Ridge, Gorge Path, West Face, or South Ridge. Another sightseeing favorite is Thunder Hole, a rock formation along Ocean Drive, where crashing waves reverberating within a small crevice create an eponymous din. The vistas from land are indeed impressive, though Charlie would encourage visitors to take to the sea. "Far fewer people see Acadia from the water, and the perspective is tremendous," he continued. "Sea kayaking is gaining popularity, and if you don't have your own kayak, there are several shops where you can rent one outside of the park. Any of the boat tours out of Bar Harbor or the other towns can be terrific too. Park naturalists narrate some of them, sharing the natural and human history as you cruise along."

It's worth noting that the 120 miles of trails that lead to some of Acadia's most jaw-dropping vistas are frequently works of art in themselves. Many were built by groups of local citizens under the auspices of organizations called village improvement societies, years before Acadia received its National Park designation. "The craftsmanship associated with the trails is unique and worthy," Charlie added. "A trail like Beachcroft has cut-granite stairs most of the way, for example. Other trails go straight up; you climb on iron rungs and walk around exposed cliffs holding on to iron railings to reach the top. [Acadia's most famous trail of this nature is Precipice. It's short—only about a mile—but you gain nearly one thousand feet over that mile, and much of it is via rungs.] The trails—as well as the carriage roads—have largely been restored to their original grandeur, thanks to the support of a nonprofit organization called Friends of Acadia. The carriage roads are a great draw for both mountain and road bikers."

There are two campgrounds in Acadia, Blackwoods (three hundred sites) and Seawall (two hundred sites). Both provide basic amenities, including picnic tables, fire rings, and potable water. Blackwoods also provides access to some special views, as Charlie describes. "You can spill out of your tent, grab a cup of coffee, and walk down to Ocean Drive within ten minutes. From here, you can watch the sunrise light up the pink granite on the seashore, but you have to really want it to get up at four or five a.m. For my money, it beats the sunrise from the top of Cadillac Mountain."

For many visitors to "down east" Maine, the trip is not complete without an opportunity to tie on a bib and tuck into a fresh lobster. In 2013 (the most recent year for which statistics are available as of this writing), more than 125 million pounds of lobster were harvested from Maine waters, with many of these succulent crustaceans coming from the cold, nutrient-rich waters off Mount Desert Island. Plated *Homarus americanus* can take infinite forms, but in these parts, locals prefer it simple—that is, steamed in shell, with sides of melted butter and lemon. Most eateries in nearby Bar Harbor feature lobster, but you needn't stray far from the trails, as lobster is on the menu at Jordan Pond House, right in the park. The original Jordan Pond House dates back more than one hundred years; the present restaurant is set up as a tea house, right on the shores of Jordan Pond. There's a big lawn in front of the house, rolling down to the pond, and people can eat outside at picnic tables. "Jordan Pond House is also known for its popovers, a tradition that goes back as long as the restaurant has been in existence," Charlie added. "The view from here is one of those classic Acadia vistas, over Jordan Pond with the Bubbles in the distance and framed by Pemetic and Penobscot Mountains. And Jordan Pond is a great starting point for some of the park's popular hiking and biking excursions. But take the Island Explorer bus to get there and other places in the park to help keep the air cleaner, better enjoy the scenery, and save yourself the trouble of finding a parking space. The bus will pick you up and drop you off right at the campground."

CHARLIE JACOBI is a natural resource specialist for Acadia National Park. He has worked for the National Park Service since 1982 and has spent the last thirty years in Acadia, focusing on managing outdoor recreation and related visitor use to ensure both protection of park resources and the quality of the visitor experience. Charlie has lead or co-lead efforts in the park to develop and implement management plans for the Carriage Roads, the trail system, the park's climbing program, and all primary visitor sites on

DESTINATION

25

Mount Desert Island, including Cadillac. He has lectured and published widely on visitor management and has been instrumental in a long-term research program at Acadia on trail and resource management. Charlie is a founding member of Friends of Baxter State Park and has served as board president for three years and on the board of directors for eight. He was the recipient of the 2010 Guy Waterman Alpine Steward Award, which is given to a person or organization that has demonstrated a long-term commitment to protecting the physical and spiritual qualities of the Northeast's mountain wilderness.

If You Go

▶ **Getting There:** Acadia is approximately 150 miles north of Portland, which is served by many major carriers. It's about 50 miles from Bangor, which is served by American Airlines, Continental Airlines, and Delta.

▶ **Best Time to Visit:** July and August are major tourist times and offer fairly consistent weather. June and September can also be excellent times to visit. The park is open year-round.

▶ **Campgrounds:** There are two campgrounds in Acadia. Blackwoods has 300 sites, and Seawall has 200 sites. There are no electrical or water hookups for RVs; site fees are $20. Reservations are highly recommended and available through the National Recreation Service (877-444-6777; www.recreation.gov).

▶ **Activities:** Hiking, biking, kayaking, and boating.

DESTINATION

25

ASSATEAGUE ISLAND NATIONAL SEASHORE

RECOMMENDED BY **Liz Davis**

"There are two main reasons that people come to Assateague," Liz Davis began. "The first is the chance to explore the habitat of an undeveloped barrier island—an increasing rarity on the highly developed East Coast. It's such a contrast to Ocean City, Maryland, which is just across an inlet to the north. The other reason that people visit Assateague is for a chance to see the horses that roam freely here."

Assateague Island National Seashore rests on Assateague Island, a thirty-seven-mile-long barrier island off the southeastern tip of Maryland. The national seashore—some 48,000 acres, with half of its area made up of water—takes up the lion's share of the Maryland portion of the island and a small portion of the Virginia section. Another well-known preserve, Chincoteague National Wildlife Refuge, takes up the remaining southern portion of the island in Virginia. (You may recall Chincoteague from Marguerite Henry's beloved children's book, *Misty of Chincoteague*.) The first European colonists arrived at Assateague in the mid-1650s; one of their lasting impacts on the island was the horses they released to graze on the seaside grasses, horses that eventually came to represent the island in the public consciousness.

Assateague's horses are not actually wild, but feral; that is, they descended from the domestic animals the colonists brought along and have reverted to a wild state. The horses graze on saltmarsh cordgrass, saltmeadow hay, and beach grass. As all of these foodstuffs are lacking in nutrients, the horses have become shorter over the last three hundred years; they're often called ponies, though they are considered horses. The animals have a broad or bloated appearance, because they drink a great deal of water, thanks to their salty diet. In the Maryland district of the park, there are currently 101 horses. (The population is controlled through a birth control vaccine that's delivered to mares via

darts.) "The Assateague horses live in social bands, led by a stallion," Liz continued. "Each band has a home range, but there are also seasonal migrations. During the summer months, the horses move to places where the mosquitoes aren't as bad, including the beaches. Seeing the horses on the beach is a special experience. They'll think nothing of flopping on the ground and stretching out for a nap. When the bugs are really bad, the horses will walk into the surf and let the waves wash over them. In the evening, they'll move back into the marshes and brush to feed and get water. As they move to and fro, they'll frequently come through our campgrounds; after all, it's part of their terrain. Campers need to store their food properly and are prohibited from feeding or touching the animals." During the spring, fall, and winter, the Life of the Forest and Life of the Marsh Trails are good places to spy bands of Assateague horses.

Feral horses may attract campers to Assateague, but there is a host of activities available to keep everyone engaged, both on the ocean and baysides of the island. "Surf fishing is very popular," Liz described. "It's usually the best in the fall, when the bluefish and red drum are moving down the coastline, though flounder, kingfish, and croaker are caught all summer. There are a number of recreational programs that we lead on the bayside. The park service provides hands-on demonstrations on crabbing (for blue crabs) and clamming (hard-shell clams and ribbed mussels), as well as surf fishing. One of our most popular programs is the kayaking tour. We provide the kayaks, and visitors head out with a ranger to explore the coastal bays. The cost is only ten dollars; the other programs are free. Many people come to play in the surf. Water temperatures on the ocean side get into the seventies, and there is a lifeguarded beach for swimming. Surfing is also popular. The water on the bayside warms up early in the season, as it's shallow, and by May, it's great for swimming and wading."

There are three main campgrounds at Assateague Island National Seashore: a drive-in campground near the ocean, a walk-in campground near the ocean (sites are just a few hundred feet from the parking area), and a drive-in campground on the bayside. "On the ocean side, you don't have Atlantic views, but it's just over a dune," Liz added. "You certainly can hear it! Some of the sites on the bayside have bay views, some even have direct bay access. This is great if you bring a kayak." The bugs that can make summertime uncomfortable for horses can do the same for humans. "Mosquitoes are prevalent from April to October," Liz continued. "Wearing long pants and long-sleeve shirts in the morning and evening helps. Repellant helps. The mosquitoes are usually not bad on the beach

OPPOSITE:
A band of horses
on the marsh
on Assateague
Island.

DESTINATION

26

. . . but during the warmest months, biting flies are active. Again, long pants and long-sleeve shirts provides some protection, but the flies mostly ignore repellant. The best you can hope for is a good breeze."

One of Liz's most lasting Assateague memories revolves around an evening bayside paddle. "The insects were horrible until we got on the water," she recalled. "The sun went down and it got dark and calm. There were fish jumping, mussels squeaking, and herons croaking; it all sounded very loud in the dark. Then we started to see bioluminescent comb jellies and plankton. We oohed and aahed and swished our hands and paddles in the water for hours, until we were pruney and pretty loony."

LIZ DAVIS is the assistant chief of interpretation at Assateague Island National Seashore, where she's worked since 1991. Liz was a first-grade teacher before joining the National Park Service, a background that's served her well in Assateague's division of Interpretation and Education. Her entire National Park Service career has been at Assateague.

DESTINATION 26

If You Go

▶ **Getting There:** The closest commercial airport is in Norfolk, Virginia, which is served by American Airlines (800-433-7300; www.aa.com) and U.S. Airways (800-428-4322; www.usairways.com). From Norfolk, it's a roughly two-hour drive.

▶ **Best Time to Visit:** Assateague is open year-round. Summer is the most popular time to visit, though the bugs can be tough. Early fall can be very pleasant.

▶ **Campgrounds:** There are three campgrounds at Assateague Island National Seashore; each includes cold-water showers and drinking water. Sites are $25 per night during the high season, $20 in off-season. Reservations are accepted April 15 through October 15; call 877-444-6777 or visit www.recreation.gov.

▶ **Activities:** Fishing, crabbing, clamming, kayaking/canoeing, wildlife viewing, hiking, and swimming.

CLIFF AND WADE LAKES

RECOMMENDED BY **Mike Harrelson**

"I have several criteria for a prime camping place," Mike Harrelson began. "First and foremost, it should be beautiful in and of itself. I should be able to unfold a chair and be affected by the landscape, the serenity of the place. However, if you're more ADHD, you should have ample activities available. Places to fish, trails for hiking and biking. Lastly, it's nice to have enough basic infrastructure to make the spot user-friendly. It's also nice to know there's a reasonably good likelihood of finding a site once you reach the place and enough space to gather a larger group. After all, much of the joy of camping is in sharing the experience with friends. Groups are good for the kids as well. As they get older, they need more stimulation than mom and dad can generally provide. It's more fun for everyone if the kids have some friends along.

"Back in the early nineties, my wife and I landed in Bozeman, Montana with our two young children. We were camping every summer weekend within a hundred-mile radius of home, exploring lots of different places. (There was no Yelp to help guide us in the right direction!) We heard about a place called Cliff and Wade Lakes, near the upper Madison River. I'd been in the area fishing on the Madison before, so knew a little bit about the landscape, beautiful big valleys with upthrusts of alpine terrain on one side, lower mountains on the other. I liked the idea of camping by a lake—much safer with kids than a river. On our first trip we came in via the famed Three Dollar Bridge access point on the Madison. You roll over some hills and drop into this heavily forested area with two natural lakes. I knew we'd discovered something special."

Cliff and Wade Lakes are situated in the Beaverhead National Forest of southwestern Montana, roughly thirty miles from the western entrance to Yellowstone. The two lakes sit at an elevation of roughly 6,400 feet and were formed by a geologic fault. Cliff

is the larger of the two lakes measuring roughly four miles in length, and has many coves ideally suited for canoeing. Spring-fed Wade is less than two miles in length and sees more recreational use. Nonetheless, a great deal of wildlife is drawn here, including larger mammals like elk and moose and numerous nesting raptors like bald eagles, osprey, and prairie falcons. Beaver and otter are also present. In a part of the world that's renowned for its trout fishing, Cliff and Wade Lakes hold a special distinction; a former-state-record rainbow trout (more than twenty pounds) was caught in Cliff in 1952, and the current-state-record brown trout—twenty-nine pounds—came from Wade in 1966.

"If you want to fish the lakes, it's best to have a canoe or small boat," Mike continued. "It's great to have some sort of watercraft just for paddling around and seeing the sights. With a canoe, you can also load up your gear and paddle out to one of a few lakeside sites away from the campground for more of a quasi-wilderness experience. [If you don't have any water transport, motorboats, kayaks, and canoes are available for rent at Wade Creek Cabins.] If I feel like river fishing, I'm inclined to roll the five miles back to Raynolds Pass, where the West Fork of the Madison meets the main stem. This part of the river is only open to wade fishing. I'll usually bring a bike when I'm over at Cliff and Wade, as one of my favorite mountain-bike rides begins nearby—Mile Creek." [This ride skirts the Continental Divide, reaching a high point of 9,987 feet.] The lakes are pretty cold, and considering the elevation, the air is on the cool side as well. In August, there's a window of twenty days or so when you can swim comfortably. The lakes are a beautiful jade color, and one year we found a rope swing. The swimming was brilliant."

There are three campgrounds at Cliff and Wade Lakes. Wade Lake and Cliff Point Campgrounds are in proximity to the lakes, with some sites adjoining the water. Hilltop Campground sits on a ridge between the lakes. While there are no water views from Hilltop, the higher elevation affords pleasant breezes. "While the campgrounds at Cliff and Wade place you in the wilderness, you're within striking distance of some pleasant small towns," Mike said. "The classic little fly-fishing–centric town of Ennis is thirty-seven miles away. There are some great restaurants there and you can grab a shower. West of Ennis you'll find the historic towns of Virginia City and Nevada City. They're well preserved, 'not quite' ghost towns. Here you can plug into a living history of the region, like a Williamsburg of Montana. If you're looking for a more woodsy, remote base camp, you can use Cliff and Wade as a staging ground to visit Yellowstone.

OPPOSITE:
Cliff Lake
Campground
provides
Montana beauty
without the
crowds of nearby
Yellowstone.

DESTINATION

27

"Montana is a land of wide-open spaces and untrammeled landscapes," Mike reflected. "Being able to connect with such landscapes is something I've dubbed 'visual Prozac.' Yet some of these landscapes become over-loved. A bit of the magic is lost when you have to make a reservation a year in advance. Cliff and Wade Lakes are busy on the Fourth of July and Labor Day and most weekends in between. But roll in on a Monday morning, and you're likely to find a campsite."

MIKE HARRELSON began working in backpacking shops and guiding white water in his teens. He headed to Jackson, Wyoming, after completing his BA in English at Virginia Tech. There he became kayaking buddies with Yvon Chouinard, founder and owner of Patagonia. His friendship with Chouinard led him to Ventura, California, where he began a fifteen-year career with the burgeoning outdoor clothing company. During those years, Mike led Patagonia's public relations efforts, served on their creative team, and became the product line/brand director for the company's snow-sports division. Mike has since run his own successful travel PR firm and cut his teeth in both outdoor and travel journalism, writing for outlets like *Outside, Backpacker, POWDER, Bomb Snow,* and *Islands.* Based in Bozeman, Montana, Mike and his wife Cindy have two boys, Clyde and Mason, who share their love for rock climbing, skiing, and far-flung adventure.

DESTINATION

27

If You Go

▶ **Getting There:** Cliff and Wade Lakes are roughly fifty miles from West Yellowstone, which is served by Delta (800-221-1212; www.delta.com); it's two hours from Bozeman, which is served by Alaska Airlines (800-252-7522; www.alaskaair.com), Delta, and United (800-864-8331; www.united.com).

▶ **Best Time to Visit:** Cliff and Wade Lakes are open to camping year-round, though most visit from late spring to early fall.

▶ **Campgrounds:** There are three campgrounds at Cliff and Wade Lakes: Wade Lake, Cliff Point, and Hilltop. All are first come, first served; fees are $12. Pit toilets and potable water are provided.

▶ **Activities:** Fishing, hiking, boating, wildlife viewing, and swimming.

TOBACCO VALLEY

RECOMMENDED BY **Tracy McIntyre**

Montana attracts a fair share of summertime tourists seeking a chance to take in the state's big sky, trout-filled rivers, and rugged, mountainous terrain. Many visitors land in the southwest section of the state, where many of its famed rivers run and Yellowstone is in easy reach. Others will make the college town of Missoula a base for their travels. A few more choose to explore the expansive and majestic territory of Glacier National Park and the increasingly chic but still inviting ski town of Whitefish, just outside the park. Very few make it to the far northwestern corner of the state, the sparsely populated region east of the Idaho panhandle, west of Whitefish and abutting the Canadian border.

But more probably should.

"I like to joke that the town where I live is named Eureka because once you land here, you realize you've found the perfect spot," Tracy McIntyre enthused. "Here in the Tobacco Valley, you have the best of both worlds. You have primitive wilderness where you can get lost with vistas as beautiful as those in Glacier, without the touristy elements. If you get lonely, there are more-developed campgrounds where you'll find other campers. And there are small communities that give you a taste of friendly, small-town Montana."

The Tobacco Valley sits between the Whitefish Range to the east in Flathead National Forest and the Purcell Mountains in the Kootenai National Forest. The Tobacco River flows through Eureka, but the region's more significant body of water is Lake Koocanusa, a reservoir (formed by the impoundment of the Kootenai River at Libby Dam) that stretches ninety miles, extending some forty miles above the border into British Columbia. The rugged country here—mountains dotted by deep cirques and rim-rocked basins— was scoured by glaciers, much like the valleys in Glacier National Park. Most of the animals that one could encounter in Glacier—including grizzly bears, lynx, black bears, moose, wolverines, mountain lions, bighorn sheep, elk, mule deer, white-tailed deer, coyotes, and wolves—are found here as well.

There are many different camping options in the greater Tobacco Valley, suited for different camping styles. The most developed (and largest) campground is Rexford Bench, on the shores of Lake Koocanusa. Popular with water-sports enthusiasts (for obvious reasons), Rexford also offers easy hiking in the nearby forest; the Hoodoo Trail leads to eponymous impressive sandstone formations not far from camp. The species of choice for anglers at Rexford Bench is kokanee, a form of landlocked sockeye salmon. Kokanee tend to travel in schools; once you locate them in the water column, you're likely to catch more than one . . . and they're a favorite on the grill or in the smoker for fish lovers. Local ospreys and bald eagles also enjoy kokanee, and you'll often have the chance to watch these winged fishers at work while you cast. (The Kootenai below Libby Dam is celebrated as a blue-ribbon trout fishery.) If you'd prefer a smaller, less developed lake setting, consider North Dickey Lake Campground near the center of the valley. North Dickey offers picnic tables and fire grates, as well as vault toilets and potable water. There's also a nice swimming beach.

If you're seeking more solitude, you might consider a hike into the backcountry of the Ten Lakes Scenic Area. Here in the Whitefish Range, peaks climb to more than 7,500 feet, and a number of glacial lakes offer opportunities for cooling swims. In addition to pack in/pack out backcountry sites, there are two lakeside campgrounds in Ten Lakes—Big and Little Therriault—which provide basic amenities. "I lead a very complex professional life, running two businesses while working full-time," Tracy ventured. "Getting up into a place like the Ten Lakes area is about rejuvenation, about becoming me again. When I come out of the mountains on Sunday evening, I'm ready to face the week."

Though part of the reason for camping in the Tobacco Valley is the chance to evade the crowds of Glacier, visitors will do well to make a day trip to the park. You'll want to spend some time on the Going-to-the-Sun Road, which cuts across the center of the park in a west-to-east direction. The fifty-two-mile highway is frequently ranked as one of the most beautiful roads in the world, and many of the park's totem characteristics—from glacial lakes to windswept passes—are on display from its macadam. As it turns out, Going-to-the-Sun Road is also the launching point for one of Glacier's most noteworthy day hikes, the Highline Trail, which parallels the Continental Divide for seven miles. The hike is all above tree line, providing for wide-open, grand vistas. The high vantage point, unbroken by trees, makes the Highline an excellent wildlife viewing trail. Hikers almost always see mountain goats and bighorn sheep on the trail. It's also a good trail to see grizzlies from—at a comfortable distance! As you leave the park, be sure to swing into Lake McDonald Lodge for a libation, or a ride around the lake in a historic wooden tour boat.

TRACY MCINTYRE was raised in beautiful northwest Montana, spending her summers working the family farm and fishing the mountain streams. After brief stints in Wisconsin and Washington, D.C., she returned to Montana in 2004 and became the director of Eureka Rural Development Partners. In addition to her role at ERDP, Tracy recently launched her own consulting company, Rural Economic Designs, LLC. Rural Economic Designs, LLC, has given Tracy the vehicle to work across the state and Pacific Northwest in community and leadership development. She has also started Montana Memories and Events (www.mtmemories.com), a full-service event-coordination company, and is actively engaged with her father's Elk Camp Arts Gallery and Showroom (www.elkcampart.com), a western gallery. Tracy graduated from Montana State University–Bozeman with a BA in history, with an emphasis in social history.

If You Go

▶ **Getting There:** The Tobacco Valley area is roughly an hour northwest of Kalispell, which is served by Alaska Airlines (800-252-7522; www.alaskaair.com) and United (800-864-8331; www.united.com).

▶ **Best Time to Visit:** Mid-June through September; October can be beautiful, but winter weather can blow in at any time.

▶ **Campgrounds:** There are a number of campgrounds around the Tobacco Valley. These include Rexford Bench (reservations through ReserveAmerica [www.reserveamerica. com], sites from $12); Big Creek (reservations through National Recreation Reservation System at www.recreation.gov, sites from $13); North Dickey Lake (reservations through National Recreation Reservation System, sites from $12); and Big and Little Therriault Lakes (first-come, first-served sites from $5, more information at www.forestcamping. com). Only basic services are available at the latter four campgrounds.

▶ **Activities:** Boating, fishing, hiking, wildlife viewing, and swimming.

DESTINATION

28

129

NAMIB DESERT

RECOMMENDED BY **Hein Truter**

"The Namib Desert is a tough place, but a beautiful place," Hein Truter ventured. "It's the kind of landscape that can bring you to your knees, but then it brings you back up again. It's the oldest desert in the world, according to the people with the big brains, and has some of the highest dunes in the world. When you think about the amount of time it's been here [it's estimated to have been formed fifty-five million years ago], you're reminded what a small bit of sand you are in the scope of things. I've seen grown men in tears at the grandeur of the place . . . then again, it could have been because their vehicles were broken!"

The Namib Desert stretches along the entire coast of Namibia (some 1,200 miles), a large, sparsely populated nation on the southwest coast of the African subcontinent, bordered by Angola to the north, Botswana to the east, and South Africa to the south. It covers 30,000 square miles of the country and is one of the driest places on earth; in parts, less than an inch of rain falls annually. A number of hardy plants and animals have evolved to withstand the aridity, soaking up moisture from the fog that blows in from the Atlantic. One of the most curious of these is *Welwitschia mirabilis*, a low-growing shrub with only two leaves that can live more than 1,000 years.) The park is also home to oryx, jackals, baboons, and hyenas. (Conditions in most of the desert are too arid to support lions and elephants, however they are occasionally found in the more northern area known as the Skeleton Coast.)

There are no resorts or campgrounds—or for that matter, roads—in the Namib. The only way to experience the desert is via 4x4. Hein's favorite route begins in Namibia's south-central region and makes its way west to the Atlantic. "When you get to the sea after all this dryness, you can't help but be struck by the contrasts," he continued. "Much of the land we cross is controlled by the Topnaar community, the indigenous people who

OPPOSITE: Some of the dunes you'll traverse in the Namib Desert approach heights of nearly 500 feet.

DESTINATION

29

131

traditionally lived here before Europeans arrived. They now offer a finite number of concessions to tour operators to bring visitors through the desert."

The adventure through the Namib begins in Namib–Naukluft National Park (famous for the grueling seventy-two-mile Naukluft Hiking Trail) and follows the path of the German settlers that came to Namibia in the late 1800s. These settlers came in search of minerals, especially diamonds. In the Kuiseb River Canyon, red sand dunes are separated by strips of grassy plains. Combined with the white of the empty river bottom and the black of surrounding formations, the Kuiseb is a kaleidoscope of natural shades. "We pitch our first camp in the river canyon," Hein described, "and guests enjoy their first Namib dinner—a somewhat meat-oriented affair. Our guides are some of the best field cooks I've ever encountered. They'll make a *braai* (barbecue) of beef steaks, eland (a large member of the antelope family), lamb, or pork; they bring the wood in. (Guides can accommodate vegetarians and other food preferences.) On the northern side of the canyon you will find some of the most southern-growing *Welwitschia mirabilis*. This area is also a good spot to see oryx, a large antelope that's evolved to be able to survive in this harsh climate. It's amazing how fat and healthy they are, given there seems to be so little to eat. One of the most beautiful sights I've ever seen was a pair of oryx running up the dunes."

After breaking down camp, your little four-wheel-drive caravan continues west, leaving an arid environment for an even drier dune experience. "As we make our way into the dunes, you begin experiencing the vastness of the desert," Hein continued. "We're often traveling in straits—the place between tall dunes, a highway of sorts. Many dunes are nearly five hundred feet tall. As we're pushing along, there may be more sightings of oryx. Jackal are frequently observed too. Part of the thrill of this adventure is negotiating the dunes. Our guides are seasoned drivers and will show you how it's done. Many visitors who want to bail out after climbing the dunes on day one will be very comfortable by the end. If adult visitors would like, they can try their hand at driving. The first challenge is learning to get over the lip of the dunes. Your instinct is to press the brake as you reach the top since you don't know what's on the other side. Do that, you'll get stuck on the belly of the vehicle. You have to get the timing just right to keep the car moving and just drop over the other side. When you're heading down, the idea is to let the car brake itself by keeping it in low gear. If you press the brakes, the back of the car will slide out, and the only way you can right it is to go faster. The night camping in the dunes is very special. The sunset is incredible; the depth and shades really shine through. We host a few photography groups each year, who come to get these shots . . . though one leading photographer who's been here has said that there's no way a camera can take in the experience."

As the caravan moves toward the coast, you'll reach the deserted diamond-mining settlements of Holsatia, Charlottenfelder, and Grillenberger. "These settlements are in one of the more inhospitable areas to live in the world," Hein mused. "No water, no supplies. Everything had to be brought in from the coastline by ox cart for the first fifteen years of exploration. It's a testament to the hardships people will endure to chase their dreams and lady luck. I don't think the land met their expectations." You'll finally reach the coast near Sandwich Harbour and Conception Bay. The wind here is stronger, and this is evidenced by the wreck of the *Eduard Bohlen*. The ship ran aground on a sand bank in the ocean. Today, it's a few hundred yards inland. "The desert is a living, evolving thing," Hein added. "A dune that's passable today may not be passable in two weeks." The *braais* of the previous evenings are replaced by a *potjie* (stew made in cast-iron pots) as the wind makes barbecuing less practical. But the wind also brings cooler temperatures.

The last day's drive toward Walvis Bay holds some of the adventure's most memorable moments. You'll pass large flocks of flamingoes and pelicans and vast colonies of fur seals. "There will usually be jackals standing among the seals, waiting for weaker ones to expire," Hein described. "It's a strange symbiosis." You'll also experience some of the trip's most intrepid driving, including Lange Wand—or "Death Acre." "Lange Wand is a very narrow stretch of beach where the dunes come right down to the sea," Hein described. "You can only pass at low tide, and it's barely two meters wide. Many have had their calculations wrong and their vehicles lost."

Hein's team have yet to lose a vehicle in Lange Wand.

HEIN TRUTER is the CEO of Live the Journey's branch in Namibia. A seasoned traveler, he has lived many years in Southeast Asia and the Middle East, however his love for the outdoors finally brought him back to Africa. Hein firmly believes that there is more to traveling than just seeing landscapes from the inside of a vehicle. "Living locally," even just for a week, is the only way to appreciate what a country and its people are about. Live the Journey (www.livethejourney.co.za) is a Southern Africa–based Destination Management Company (DMC) that offers more than thirty unique destinations to the more adventurous traveler. This includes gorilla trekking in Rwanda, snow golf in Mongolia, driving monster trucks in Iceland, or tracking desert lions in Namibia!

If You Go

► **Getting There:** International travelers generally enter Namibia via the capital, Windhoek, which is served from Europe by Air Namibia (+264-61-2996000; www.airnamibia.com) and from South Africa by British Airways (800-247-9297; www.britishairways.com) and South African Airways (800-722-9675; www.flysaa.com).

► **Best Time to Visit:** Tours of the Namib are offered year-round. Hein recommends that you avoid Easter season and June/July, as this is high season for South African vacationers. Spring and fall are a bit cooler, though temperatures are not as extreme as you'd imagine.

► **Campgrounds:** Faces of the Namib Tours (www.facesofthenamib.com) has one of the few concessions to lead tours and camping in the region described above and will handle all the gear.

► **Activities:** Wildlife viewing, four-wheel driving.

DESTINATION

29

RIO CHAMA

RECOMMENDED BY **Stephen Bohannon**

"I came out to New Mexico from Indiana following a woman," Stephen Bohannon reminisced. "It turned out that she was the wrong woman, but she brought me to the right state. My first trip to Rio Chama struck home the splendor of New Mexico. I left Albuquerque at eleven at night and drove north, accompanied through the deep darkness by a silvery full moon. We set up camp late that night above the river and went to sleep. I woke up to an amazing display of color and was blown away by the scope and scale of the rocks around me. I went from a desaturated landscape to a place awash in Technicolor."

The Rio Chama begins in Colorado and flows roughly 130 miles through northern New Mexico before reaching the Rio Grande north of Santa Fe. The section of the river that's of greatest interest to recreationists is the 31-mile segment that flows out of El Vado Dam into the Santa Fe National Forest and the Chama River Canyon Wilderness, above Abiquiú Dam. Rafters and kayakers come from far and wide to float through multicolored sandstone canyons that soar to heights eclipsing 1,500 feet. Here, paddling enthusiasts can experience all the grandeur that's summed up in New Mexico's slogan, "Land of Enchantment." "The stretch of river above Abiquiú is not too scary, in terms of rapids," Stephen continued. "There are some Class IIs and Class IIIs, but nothing too daunting. The real appeals are the tremendous vistas and the chance to explore the many side canyons. The cliff faces are like a giant scoop of Neapolitan ice cream—shifting layers of red, cream, and brown. It seems that there's another vibrant rock formation around every bend. The side canyons on this stretch of river are another great attraction. It's very worthwhile to tie up your raft or kayak at these canyons and do some exploring for Native American artifacts. Almost all of the canyons have petroglyphs (rock engravings made by removing a portion of rock surface by incising or carving); many have pottery shards or

flakes from the creation of arrowheads. It's a very rich cultural area. (No artifacts should be removed from the canyons, of course.) In one spot, called Dark Canyon, there are dinosaur tracks in the sandstone, probably those of a hadrosaur [a duck-billed dinosaur]."

In addition to fine paddling, this section of Rio Chama is considered one of New Mexico's best-kept secrets for trout anglers. Brown trout are the main target here, with fish averaging twelve to eighteen inches. The state's record brown trout—20.5 pounds—came from these fertile waters in 1946. Animal life above the water is equally plentiful along the wooded canyons of Rio Chama and includes elk, mule deer, and black bear.

Some people will float the entire wilderness section of Rio Chama over several days, camping along the river. For those wishing to do day floats, there are a number of options along the lower stretches of the river. "Forest Road 151 joins the river near the Big Eddy Boat Take-out and parallels the Chama for twelve or fifteen miles," Stephen explained. "At Big Eddy, there's a no-frills Forest Service campground. There's no potable water or hook-ups, but the views are beautiful and some of the sites are right on the water. There are a number of unofficial camping spots along the road further upstream, where you can set up a tent or smaller RV. Many times, I'll come in on a Friday night and set up a little camp in this section. I'll arrange for a shuttle driver to take me and my kayak upstream in the morning. When I come off the river, I'm right at my camp and it's already set up."

Given northern New Mexico's incredible color palette and play of light, it's no surprise that many painters have been drawn to the region. Perhaps none of the region's artists are better known than Georgia O'Keeffe. O'Keeffe had garnered attention for her iconoclastic renderings of flowers and cityscapes while living in New York, but is best remembered for her at times surreal paintings of the Southwest—many, like *Summer Days*, featuring a motif of deer, cattle, or ram skulls. She first visited the Rio Chama area—specifically Ghost Ranch, which had been established as a retreat—in 1934, and was so taken with the place that she eventually bought a home there in 1940 and made it her permanent residence in 1949. Today, Ghost Ranch operates as an education and retreat center. In addition to tours that highlight O'Keeffe's life and inspirations, Ghost Ranch also offers excursions exploring the region's rich archeological and paleontological offerings. "You'll drive right past Ghost Ranch as you head toward Rio Chama," Stephen added. "It's definitely worth a stop. Further up Forest Road 151, you'll find the Monastery of Christ in the Desert. If you enjoy beer, you'll want to visit here too, as the monks grow their own hops and brew a number of products."

OPPOSITE:
Brilliantly shaded cliffs mark much of the course of the Rio Chama.

DESTINATION

30

If you make it to camp along Rio Chama, you'll want to experience Echo Amphitheater, just north of Ghost Ranch. "It's a neat escarpment that was formed in the colorful sandstone," Stephen described. "There's a paved trail that leads to the natural amphitheater. All vocalizations are echoed back to you. You can only imagine what significance this spot must have had for indigenous people."

STEPHEN BOHANNON is *New Mexico Magazine*'s assistant art director. Though he's proud of his Louisville roots, he quickly fell in love with New Mexico. Whether he's playing disc golf, brewing craft beer, or organizing board-game meet-ups, Bohannon is elated to have landed in a state that embraces his curiosity and diverse interests. Two of his passions—graphic design and paleontology—collided in the March 2014 issue, when he illustrated the story of a boy on a hunt for traces of ancient life ("The Land of the Giants," www.mynm.us/nmdinos). Stephen serves on the board of the Albuquerque Wildlife Federation and helps run volunteer efforts to restore and create wetland habitats. He calls New Mexico's wilderness the "connective tissue" that binds him to the state—especially the Gila, the world's oldest protected wilderness area, where he enjoys backpacking to Jordan Hot Springs.

If You Go

▶ **Getting There:** The town of Abiquiú is roughly two hours north of Albuquerque, which is served by most major carriers.

▶ **Best Time to Visit:** Summers can be quite warm in the high desert around Abiquiú and Rio Chama, so many visitors prefer spring and early fall.

▶ **Campgrounds:** Both the established campground along the Rio Chama and the less formal sites are very basic, with no potable water provided. Sites are free and available on a first-come, first-served basis. Campers should bring everything they need. Sites with more amenities are available at nearby Ghost Ranch (505-685-4333; www.ghostranch.org).

▶ **Activities:** Boating, fishing, hiking/backpacking, wildlife viewing, and cultural tours at Ghost Ranch. If you plan to do any paddling, Up the Creek Shuttle (at 575-588-7704) can transport you and your raft/kayak upstream (or your automobile downstream).

ADIRONDACK PARK

RECOMMENDED BY **Karin Tate**

"After my first few trips out west, I was a bit worried about what it would be like to be back in the Adirondacks," Karin Tate ventured. "The landscapes there are gorgeous, awe-inspiring. The Adirondacks are more intimate; the landscape is not as grand and imposing. It's more welcoming. The mountains here are not in ranges per se, but jumbled together, with many lakes in between. For me, the landscape creates an enfolding kind of experience. It's easy to understand why so many people fall in love with the area."

Adirondack Park encompasses more than six million acres of northeastern New York State—much of the area north of a line that would stretch from above the state capital in Albany, west to Utica. (It comprises the largest publicly protected area in the contiguous United States, the equivalent of Yosemite, Yellowstone, Glacier, the Grand Canyon, and the Great Smokies National Parks combined.) The park is a unique pastiche of private lands, state-owned wilderness areas, and more than 100 small towns, replete with forty-two 4,000-plus-foot peaks, 3,000 lakes and ponds, 30,000 miles of white-water rivers and gurgling trout streams, and 2,000 miles of hiking trails and the headwaters of the mighty Hudson.

The park is divided into seven geographical regions: the Adirondack Wild, Lake George Region, Adirondack Coast, Adirondack Lakes, Lake Placid, Adirondacks–Tug Hill, and the Adirondack Seaway. Each has its special appeals, but wherever you go, water activities and hiking are likely to be on the trip's agenda. "There are so many lakes and ponds in the Adirondacks, you can really have some great canoeing adventures," Karin continued. "In the southern part of the park, many of the lakes are connected and you can paddle from one to the other. In the north, you have the beginning of the Northern Forest Canoe Trail, which goes seven hundred and forty miles from Saranac

Lake to Fort Kent, Maine, passing through Vermont, Québec, and New Hampshire along the way." The trail follows old Native American travel routes. Though acid rain impacted many of the Adirondacks' fisheries some decades ago, many rivers and lakes have bounced back, offering healthy populations of wild trout, as well as smallmouth bass, northern pike, and walleye.

"There are infinite opportunities for hikers, whether along forested trails to hidden lakes or to mountain peaks," Karin said. "There's a club called the Forty-Sixers, whose members strive to climb the forty-six highest peaks in the Adirondacks. [Early climbers Robert and George Marshall arrived at the number forty-six thinking that this was the number of mountain peaks that eclipsed four thousand feet; modern surveys showed that four of the original forty-six are actually just under four thousand feet in elevation.] I've hiked quite a few of them. I remember being on top of Cascade Mountain once, one of the forty-six peaks—and not too hard to reach. From the top, you have a three-hundred-and-sixty-degree view of the entire high-peaks area. On a clear day, you can see all the way to the White Mountains in New Hampshire, two states away!"

Wherever you are in the Adirondacks, camping opportunities abound. There are more than a hundred campgrounds and thousands of campsites waiting. "Most of the state-run campgrounds cater to tent campers," Karin continued. "RVers will find hook-ups and other services at commercial campgrounds. If you're looking for a more isolated camping experience, there are many primitive lakeside sites that can be reached by canoe or kayak. And for backpackers, Adirondack Park has an extensive network of lean-tos: two hundred in all. These lean-tos are three-sided structures made of logs, available on a first-come, first-served basis." If you opt for campgrounds a little closer to civilization, many small-town charms await, be it a community-band concert or a homemade ice-cream cone. "In some communities, like Saranac Lake, people have been coming up forever for vacations," Karin added. "For the most part, it's not a fancy place. You find people from all walks of life up there, and everything is low-key . . . a quality I love."

In her role as a national outings leader for the Sierra Club, Karin has designed itineraries to showcase the natural beauty and recreational opportunities available in the Adirondacks. She shared the details of one five-day itinerary, based at a campground near the center of the park, outside of the village of Indian Lake. "On the first day, I'll take visitors on a hike—perhaps on a section of Northville–Placid Trail, which runs one hundred thirty-three miles through some of the wildest sections of the Adirondack. The second day, we'll

OPPOSITE:
Adirondack Park
boasts more than
3,000 lakes and
ponds, many
of which have
surrounding
campsites.

DESTINATION

31

take to the water with an all-day kayak trip on one of the beautiful lakes in the area. On day three, I like to visit Great Camp Santanoni, one of the estates (or "great camps") that were built by wealthy downstaters at the turn of the last century. [It's considered one of the greatest examples of Adirondack craftsmanship.] The next day, we'll explore some of the great white water the area has to offer. There's a seventeen-mile stretch of the Indian and Hudson Rivers that I've run in the past in a raft (with skilled guides) that has some solid Class III rapids, plus some quieter pools where you can swim."

If you find yourself in the central region of Adirondack Park, consider a visit to the Adirondack Museum in the village of Blue Mountain Lake. The museum has an extensive collection of boats inspired by the region's myriad waterways and does an excellent job of chronicling the legacy of outdoor recreation in the mountains.

KARIN TATE serves as a national outings leader for the Sierra Club. Before joining the Sierra Club, she taught mathematics at the Winsor School in Boston. A Sierra Club member since 1976, her outside adventures include hiking the Appalachian Trail (March–September, 1986), the French and German Alps, and the Cascades.

If You Go

► **Getting There:** The closest commercial airports are in Syracuse and Albany, both roughly two and a half hours away. Both are served by most major domestic carriers.

► **Best Time to Visit:** Campgrounds are generally open from mid-May to mid-October. Summer months are the busiest; black flies can be thick in the early season, September can be beautiful.

► **Campgrounds:** The fifty-two state campgrounds within Adirondack Park are overseen by the New York State Department of Environmental Conservation (www.dec.ny.gov). Reservations for many of the campgrounds can be made through ReserveAmerica (www.newyorkstateparks.reserveamerica.com). Site prices begin at $20. The many privately operated campgrounds in the area are listed at Visit Adirondacks (www.visitadirondacks.com).

► **Activities:** Hiking, canoeing, white-water rafting, swimming, fishing, rock climbing, sightseeing.

ABEL TASMAN NATIONAL PARK

RECOMMENDED BY **Hugh and Pam Mytton**

Many know the southern island of New Zealand for its mountains and fjords, its rushing rivers and adrenaline-fueled outdoor sports. Abel Tasman National Park's wonders are on a bit of a smaller scale, but are nonetheless beguiling. Resting near the top of the south island, the park extends from Wainui Inlet in the north to Marahau in the south and includes the waters of the Tonga Island Marine Reserve. Though Abel Tasman is New Zealand's smallest national park (at eighty-seven square miles), it is its most popular, visited by more than 150,000 hikers, beachgoers, campers, and kayakers each year. The first time you set your eyes upon its golden sand beaches, you'll understand why! Two well-known tracks (trails) traverse the park, one cutting through the rolling terrain of the interior, one along the coast. Kayakers have mapped out another trail of sorts along the coastline, where some visitors will paddle the length of the park over three or four days, camping along the way.

One of the great appeals of Abel Tasman—which is named for the Dutch explorer who is believed to be the first European to set eyes upon modern-day New Zealand—is the park's tremendous diversity of habitat. There are imposing rocky headlands, river estuaries and lagoons filled with clear water, and the aforementioned beaches. In places, thick forests extend right to the shoreline, creating a vivid contrast of green, gold, and blue. Along the northern coast of the park, you're likely to find fur seals; further south, there are rookeries of blue penguins, the smallest member of the penguin species. For many, the relaxing ambiance of Totaranui Campground has enough appeal in itself. "We get some visitors who are traveling through the country and might stop for a night or two," began Hugh Mytton. "Other campers come for two or three weeks. We'll get people who have stressful jobs—solicitors, bankers—they arrive, put on shorts and T-shirts, and

143

relax. It's so nice to see them enjoying themselves." "Many people live in cities, and their lives are very busy," Pam Mytton chimed in. "Coming here, people have time for one another. They get into a different rhythm. Though there are many attractions around the national park, many of our visitors don't wander far from the campground."

Totaranui Campground provides an exceptional base for exploring Abel Tasman National Park . . . or for simply kicking back. Accessed by a seven-mile gravel road, it sits between Totaranui Beach and a large estuary. The big golden beach (the color is a result of a high percentage of orthoclase minerals in the sand) and crystalline waters on either side of the tent/caravan sites are a great draw. "There are three things that children love," Hugh continued. "Water, mud, and fire. Totaranui delivers all three. The estuary is a lovely spot for younger children. The water—a beautiful blue-green color—is a bit warmer than the sea off the beach, and there's not much current. It's perfect for splashing about and making sand castles. As for the fire—kids can roast marshmallows around the fire pit in the evening. There are also some easy walks that depart from the campground. The Pukatea Walk is just thirty minutes, but it will give you a great sense of the plants and birds of the New Zealand bush." The trail takes walkers through a number of different habitats, including gorse scrubland, a raupo (bulrush) swamp, and a pukatea forest with glades of nīkau palms (the only palm endemic to New Zealand) and black mamaku tree ferns. You may spy some of the South Island's inland avian residents, including tui, bell-bird, and kererū. (Kiwi, the flightless bird that's most closely associated with New Zealand, is not endemic to the region. A population of great spotted kiwi exists to the northwest, though the long-term well-being of these birds—like other kiwi populations in New Zealand—is in question, thanks to predation by mammals that have been introduced to the islands.)

Frequent visitors to Totaranui may be content to enjoy the immediate environs of the campground. But those from further afield may wish to do some exploring. While there are no roads along the water, several fleets of water taxis await to spirit you up and down the coastline. "You can arrange to catch a boat south," Hugh explained. "You can then hike back to the campground, or you can arrange to be picked up where you're dropped off or some-where else along the coast. Outings can be arranged to accommodate many different tastes and activity levels." Heading north, you might opt to explore Golden Bay and the granite headland of Separation Point. There's a sizable New Zealand fur seal colony here, and you can hike down to observe them. (Fur seals are not true seals, as they have external ears and

OPPOSITE:
Golden beaches
and turquoise
seas are just
two of the many
attractions at
Abel Tasman.

DESTINATION

32

forward-rotating hind flippers. They're in the same family as sea lions.) If you opt to taxi south, you might visit Anchorage Bay. From here, you can hike to the overlook at Te Pukatea Bay, which provides vistas all the way across Tasman Bay. Or, you can visit Cleopatra's Pool, a freshwater swimming hole that comes with a moss-lined, natural waterslide. Another nearby attraction is a glowworm cave, lit by thousands of *Arachnocampae luminosa*, an iridescent worm endemic to New Zealand. There's also the option of boating to Adele Island, where mammals have been eradicated and native bird species have been reintroduced. From the beach, you can close your eyes and take in an avian symphony. Blue penguins are sometimes spied swimming the calm waters around Adele.

Even if you have limited experience captaining a kayak, you should consider at least a morning or afternoon paddle along the shorelines, lagoons, and estuaries of Abel Tasman. The water along most of the coastline is quite calm, and guides are available if you have any trepidation about being on the water. Your reward will be a richer perspective of the shoreline and a dazzling display of color beneath the surface. Pink algae coats the rocks in protected waters, providing a bright backdrop for a host of smaller creatures, ranging from periwinkles, tube worms, Neptune's necklace (also known as sea grapes), sea urchins, and Cook's turban shells. You'll glide past a host of waterbirds, like shags, oyster-catchers, herons, and pūkeko (purple swamphen) and may even spy dolphins. Bigger surprises might await you—Hugh has come upon pods of orcas sweeping into the shallows to feed on stingrays!

HUGH AND PAM MYTTON are Totaranui's only permanent inhabitants, and they manage the Department of Conservation campground at Abel Tasman National Park. Hugh is a passionate rugby fan, and he enjoys bird watching, fishing, and hunting. Pam enjoys family time with her new granddaughter, as well as bush walking and gardening. Off-season, the Myttons enjoy traveling with their family to the South Pacific.

If You Go

▶ **Getting There:** Most visitors will fly into Nelson, which is served via Auckland, Christchurch, and Wellington by Air New Zealand (+64 9 357 3000; www.airnewzealand. co.nz). Marahau, near Abel Tasman National Park, is a ninety-minute drive from Nelson.

DESTINATION

32

► **Best Time to Visit:** Most visitors paddle between October and mid-April, with the austral summer being the busiest season.

► **Campgrounds:** Totaranui Campground (within the park) can accommodate up to 850 campers and provides flush toilets, potable water, cold showers, and fire pits. Reservations can be made by calling +64 3 528 8083 or visiting www.doc.govt.nz. Fees in the high season are $15 (NZD).

► **Activities:** Hiking, swimming, kayaking, fishing.

DESTINATION

32

GREATER QUEENSTOWN

RECOMMENDED BY **Dave Macleod**

"I was drawn to Queenstown in the early nineties because there was lots of rock around, but not much of an infrastructure for climbers," Dave Macleod recalled. "I saw an opportunity to develop rock climbing as a pastime. At that time, Queenstown had a few nice bars and one movie theater. Now it has two theaters, two casinos, and a hundred bars. When I leave to go to work, people are making their way home from the night before! Though it's grown, Queenstown has a tremendous energy. The views take your breath away when you land here. It's like Whistler or Interlaken, Switzerland, just an abundance of geographical features. And it's such a great base for all forms of outdoor activities—mountain biking, road biking, climbing, hiking, rafting, fishing—the list goes on! Ten minutes from town, you can be by yourself. It's so easy to escape into the backcountry from Queenstown."

Queenstown rests along the shores of crystal-clear, mountain-bordered Lake Wakatipu, in the southwest corner of the South Island of New Zealand. Near the heart of the Otago region, it's tucked between Mount Aspiring National Park (to the north), Fiordland National Park (to the south), and Milford Sound (to the west). Peter Jackson's *Lord of the Rings* trilogy showed the world what most Kiwis already knew—that this region is an area of incomparable natural beauty. (Moviegoers will recognize many scenes from Middle Earth upon touching down there!) The combination of steep mountains, dark-green forests, snow-capped peaks, foaming waterfalls, and fingers of blue fjords make the region one of the most visually stunning temperate areas in the world. The region is home to what many consider to be the world's most beautiful hike, the Milford Track. Anglers regularly make the pilgrimage to the South Island to fish its clear, uncrowded streams. Wineries are thriving in this former gold-mining area. And, as you may recall, bungee jumping was conceived there.

OPPOSITE: Many campers visiting New Zealand will rent RVs to explore the lakes and mountains around Queenstown.

DESTINATION

(33)

Cape Breton Highlands is celebrated for its rich assemblage of half-day hikes. One can take a pleasant nature walk in the morning, have lunch in a Celtic pub, and do another modest hike in the afternoon. One relatively short but saucy trail is Franey, on the east side of the park. It climbs 1,400 feet in two miles, but you're rewarded at the top with splendid views of the town of Ingonish, the Clyburn Valley, and Franey Mountain behind, and the open Atlantic before you, with Middle Head Peninsula jutting right below, out into the sea. Middle Head Trail, which starts near the historic Keltic Lodge, is a finger that extends into the Atlantic and offers great ocean views and vistas of Ingonish Island. Many people like to visit the lodge, have lunch, and then walk Middle Head, which takes less than two hours. (The adjoining golf course, Highlands Links, opened in 1941 and was designed by the celebrated golf designer Stanley Thompson. The course was commissioned by the Canadian National Park Service to attract visitors in the waning years of the Great Depression and is considered one of Canada's top courses and one of Thompson's masterpieces.) "The Middle Head Trail has some great picnicking spots too," Mariève continued. "You can watch the gannets dive, maybe see a whale if you're lucky." Hiking is so popular in Cape Breton that the island conducts the ten-day Hike the Highlands Festival each September, which hosts guided hikes and programs of interest to hikers.

There are five front-country campgrounds in Cape Breton Highlands National Park. The two largest are Broad Cove (on the east side of the park, with 202 sites) and Chéticamp (on the west side, with 117 sites). Broad Cove is set a short walk from the Atlantic near the village of Ingonish and offers both tent sites and RV sites (with hookups), plus hot showers and kitchen shelters. Chéticamp Campground is nestled between the mountains and the Chéticamp River, not far from the village of Chéticamp and from beaches, and offers the same amenities available at Broad Cove. Both Broad Cove and Chéticamp offer five oTENTiks, a spacious blend of tent and rustic cabin equipped with beds and furniture on a raised floor, for people easing into camping. "My personal favorite in the park is Corney Brook Campground," Mariève shared. "It's right off the Cabot Trail, so it's very accessible, but it's very intimate. The sites are right by the ocean, and there's a private beach. You have the mountains to the east and can watch the sun set over the Gulf of St. Lawrence. It's the best of both worlds." For people who have little camping experience, Cape Breton Highlands National Park offers a "Learn to Camp" weekend. Novices can learn how to set up a tent, make a campfire, and cook outdoors, among other camping basics.

OPPOSITE:
The Cabot Trail,
which cuts
through Cape
Breton Highlands
National Park,
is regularly
recognized as
one of the world's
most beautiful
roads.

DESTINATION

34

There are also hikes and campfire activities. "It's a great way for new campers to learn about camping and gain confidence, as there's the support of park employees and other novices," Mariève added. (Like several other Canadian national parks, Cape Breton Highlands National Park also offers equipped camping. Visitors just show up with food and bedding; everything else is provided.)

Part of the allure of a visit to Cape Breton is a chance to partake of the region's thriving Celtic culture. With strong Mi'kmaq and French cultures, Cape Breton Island has also been shaped by Scottish immigrants, who arrived in the early 1800s. (Oddly enough, geologists believe that Cape Breton may have initially been connected to Scotland millions of years ago!) These Scots, forcibly displaced from the Scottish Highlands, have managed to maintain much of their way of life. While the number of citizens speaking Gaelic is shrinking, the region's culture is being passionately preserved in its music, especially a style of violin playing that's been branded "Cape Breton Fiddling," characterized by such artists as Natalie MacMaster. The region's music and scenic beauty are celebrated with Celtic Colours, an island-wide festival held each October.

Cape Breton Highlands National Park interpreters lead a number of activities throughout the summer season. One of the most popular is the Skyline Sunset Hike. "The Skyline trail is relatively flat and not too long—about five miles to the end and back," Mariève described. "You head through the boreal forest, and when you reach the end, you're at the top of a mountain that falls off more than thirteen hundred feet to the Gulf of St. Lawrence. Interpreters begin the hike two hours before sunset so you reach the headland just as the sun is dropping. Sometimes you'll see whales down below from the boardwalk at the trail's end. It's not uncommon to see moose or black bear from this trail, though the bears are generally on a distant hillside. The interpreter leads the way back, and you reach your car by dark."

MARIÈVE THERRIAULT has been working with Parks Canada since the year 2000. For the past ten years, she has worked at Cape Breton Highlands National Park, first as a park interpreter and now as the product development officer, where she leads new projects to build on the park's inventory of memorable visitor experiences. Mariève is an avid hiker and trail runner.

DESTINATION

34

If You Go

▶ **Getting There:** Air Canada (888-247-2262; www.aircanada.com) offers daily flights to Halifax, Nova Scotia, from a number of North American cities, with connecting flights to Sydney, which is on the island. Travelers can also reach Yarmouth, Nova Scotia, via boat from Portland, Maine (800-845-4073; www.scotiaprince.com) or Bar Harbor (888-249-7245; www.catferry.com). From Halifax, it's roughly a five-hour drive to Ingonish, at the southeastern edge of the park. From Sydney, it's two hours.

▶ **Best Time to Visit:** July through September is the most popular time to camp. October can be beautiful, but there's potential for wintry weather as the month goes on. Campgrounds are open from mid-May to mid-October.

▶ **Campgrounds:** There are five front-country backgrounds in Cape Breton Highlands. Reservations are accepted at Chéticamp and Broad Cove campgrounds through Parks Canada (877-737-3783; www.reservation.pc.gc.ca); other campgrounds are first come, first served. Sites range from $17.60 to $38.20 (CAD).

▶ **Activities:** Hiking, swimming, sightseeing, fishing, cycling, and golf.

DESTINATION

34

PUKASKWA NATIONAL PARK

RECOMMENDED BY **Annique Maheu**

Annique Maheu recalled her first visit to Pukaskwa National Park. "I had been working with Parks Canada, the Canadian park service, in the Northwest Territories, above the Arctic Circle, and was heading back home to Ontario to visit my family. I decided to stop in Pukaskwa to visit some colleagues. It was dark when I arrived. In the morning, I was blown away by the beauty of the place. I'd heard the north coast of Lake Superior described as "the wild shores of an inland sea," and that seemed spot on. Lake Superior is such a massive body of water; it's a being on its own. My first visit was in August, and it was the height of blueberry season. It was astonishing to see so many plants in bloom in a place that can be so harsh. I hadn't expected to encounter such a sense of wildness in my home province."

Pukaskwa encompasses 725 square miles of rugged boreal forest along Lake Superior, roughly 250 miles northwest of Sault Ste. Marie. Though it's Ontario's largest national park, Pukaskwa sees only 10,000 visitors a year. The terrain here is emblematic of the Canadian Shield, the geological core that encompasses half of Canada, and is typified by coniferous forests interspersed with expanses of igneous rock. Pukaskwa is also Ontario's largest designated national wilderness park, and its untrammeled forests are home to moose, black bears, beavers, and gray wolves. (It's believed that a small population of woodland caribou inhabit the park, though the herd's numbers have fluctuated.) There's some debate about the derivation of the name. According to one of the legends of the Ojibway people who historically have called this region home, a man had a fight with his wife at the mouth of a river near the southern edge of the park. He killed her, burned her body, and tossed the charred bones into the river. He was given the name *Opakasu* which means "cooker of marrow," and the river became known as the Pukasu, thanks to his deed. Pukaskwa is an anglicization of Pukasu.

OPPOSITE: Visitors to Pukaskwa can hike to many inland lakes like this and along the "inland sea," namely Lake Superior.

DESTINATION

35

159

"People come to Pukaskwa for several reasons," Annique continued. "Harder-core outdoor enthusiasts come to have a rugged wilderness experience, whether it be hiking the thirty-six-mile Coastal Hiking Trail or paddling along the coast in Lake Superior on the Coastal Paddling Route. If you're looking for a backcountry experience, this is the best place in the province of Ontario. [There are a number of primitive campsites along the Coastal Trail and Paddling Route that come equipped with a tent pad, privy, bear box, and fire pit.] But we also have people who visit to have a taste of the Canadian wilderness with a certain level of comfort. You can camp at Hattie Cove [near the northwest edge of the park] with warm showers and flush toilets; some sites have electricity as well, for RVs. The great Canadian wilderness is at the other side of your tent zipper, but you can come back in the evening to some nice amenities."

A chance to commune with Lake Superior, the largest of the Great Lakes, is a big draw for many Pukaskwa visitors. It can be an unfriendly body of water, as anyone who's heard Gordon Lightfoot's "The Wreck of the Edmund Fitzgerald" can attest. Even in the summer the water is cold, hovering in the low forties, though warmer pockets can be found behind the islands, making ideal swimming spots. The lake's cold temperatures have the effect of creating a microclimate, resulting in the presence of many arctic plants near the park. Intrepid kayakers and canoeists will paddle the entire coastline—more than one hundred miles—usually beginning from Hattie Cove and working south. Kayaking the coast exposes you to the tremendous geology of the region, but it's only recommended for more-seasoned paddlers. (Naturally Superior Adventures from Wawa, Ontario, leads trips along the Pukaskwa coast.) If you're looking for a gentler way to experience a taste of paddling the big lake, the inlets of Hattie Cove offer a safe and manageable alternative. A slightly less challenging way to experience Lake Superior is to hike a portion of the Coastal Hiking Trail. The hike to the White River Suspension Bridge is demanding at eleven miles, but you won't soon forget the views from the bridge, which sits seventy-five feet above Chigamiwinigum Falls.

"I did the hike to White River one fall," Annique shared. "There's a point where the trail meets the river. It's a massive canyon at this point, and the river is just bursting to get to Lake Superior. You can almost feel the rapids from above. The whole hike is a true Pukaskwa experience. You leave the campground on the shores of Lake Superior, hike through an area of prescribed fire where the forest is regenerating, through a large wetland, then you go deep into the boreal forest. Finally you come to a breathtaking vista of a river rushing through. It's a chance to encounter true wilderness in a very accessible manner."

There is a host of less-arduous ways to connect with the spirit of Pukaskwa. One is to visit the Anishinaabe encampment near the center of the park. Here, a First Nations interpreter is on hand to explain and demonstrate facets of the Ojibway culture. You can even take part in the occasional smudge ceremony, where native grasses are burned and participants can cleanse their bodies and minds in a time-honored tradition. Pukaskwa also hosts an active geocaching program; this GPS-driven treasure hunt helps you experience both the cultural and ecological facets of the park at your own pace. The park's new Xplorers program for children ages six to eleven also offers a unique and exciting way to discover the park through engaging activities and adventures.

ANNIQUE MAHEU is an avid French-Canadian outdoor enthusiast who loves hiking, paddling, camping, and mountain biking and has a passion for Canada's true north and near north. She started working for Parks Canada as a university student in 2004 and has since loved working for Parks Canada at various national historic sites and national parks across the country. Annique now serves as the visitor experience manager at Pukaskwa National Park.

If You Go

► **Getting There:** Visitors can fly into Sault Ste. Marie, Michigan/Ontario, which is served by several carriers, including Air Canada (888-247-2262; www.aircanada.com) and Delta (800-221-1212; www.delta.com). From here, it's roughly 250 miles to Pukaskwa.

► **Best Time to Visit:** The season is May to September, though bugs can be aggressive in the earlier months; August and September can be glorious.

► **Campgrounds:** Hattie Cove has sixty-seven sites, twenty-nine of which have electricity. Sites here in the summer season begin at $25.50 (CAD); backcountry sites are $19.50 (CAD).

► **Activities:** Hiking, paddling, swimming, fishing, cultural exchange.

CRATER LAKE NATIONAL PARK

RECOMMENDED BY **Brian Ettling**

"Growing up, I had pictures of many national parks in my room—including Crater Lake," Brian Ettling recalled. "It was an inspiring image, though far, far away. In my teens, I had the chance to visit Vancouver, British Columbia, when my high school band was chosen to play at the World's Fair. I fell in love with the Pacific Northwest and knew I wanted to live there one day. When I graduated from college, I found a job listing for the gift shop at Crater Lake National Park. I still remember the day I arrived—May 20, 1992—and it was love at first sight. Twenty-two years later, that love affair hasn't stopped."

Crater Lake National Park sits in the Cascade Mountains of southern Oregon, roughly an hour north of the city of Klamath Falls. The lake itself rests at the bottom of a six-mile-wide, 8,000-foot-tall caldera. Shimmering in hues of incredible blue at the bottom of a crater that varies from 500 to nearly 2,000 feet in depth, the lake is wonder-of-the-world inspiring; your first glimpse may leave you speechless. There are two stories of how Crater Lake came to be. The Klamath people, one of the Native American tribes that call the region home, tell a legend of two chiefs, Llao of the Below-World and Skell of the Above-World. They became pitted in a battle that ended up in the destruction of Llao's home, 12,000-plus-foot-tall Mount Mazama. The mountain's destruction led to the creation of Crater Lake. Geologists believe that an ancient volcano (posthumously named Mount Mazama) erupted. The basin or caldera was formed after the top 5,000 feet of the volcano collapsed. Subsequent lava flows sealed the bottom, allowing the caldera to fill with approximately 4.6 trillion gallons of water from rainfall and snowmelt, creating the ninth-deepest lake in the world.

"Though it sounds cliché, the first thing that strikes you about Crater Lake is its pure-blue hue," Brian continued. "It just blows your mind, especially when it's calm in the

OPPOSITE:
Crater Lake is the deepest lake in America, with a depth of 1,943 feet. Visitors can take a ferry to Wizard Island and leap into its incredibly blue (and cold!) waters.

DESTINATION

36

morning in the summer before the boats go out, and the sky and surrounding mountains are perfectly reflected on the surface." Many of the most popular activities at Crater Lake serve to highlight different ways to take in its beauty. Hiking is one option. "If you want to get the most bang for your buck, consider Watchman Peak," Brian said. "It's less than a mile each way and only gains about six hundred feet in elevation, but it takes you to a peak and gives you a bird's-eye view of the lake.

If you want more of a workout, consider Garfield Peak. This hike starts at Crater Lake Lodge, and goes 1.7 miles each way, but gains a thousand feet in elevation. From this vantage point you have a great view of Phantom Ship, a rock formation that suggests a schooner. Members of the Mazamas mountaineering group suggested that the lodge be located where it is so members could stop and have a cocktail and appetizer after hiking Garfield. Thanks to the elevation, it never gets very hot here in summer, rarely more than eighty degrees. So hiking is never uncomfortable.

"If visitors are less able to get around on foot, there are two-hour trolley tours that circumnavigate the thirty-three-mile loop around the rim. There are a number of amazing pullouts; it's like a theater in the round with each seat giving you a different view. There are at least eight stops when I do the tour, and I can honestly say that I don't have a favorite. I also like to highlight the rich Native American lore around Mazama." (It's worth noting that the loop that circles the lake's rim resides in many cyclists' lists of "top ten" rides.)

After taking in the lake from above, you may wish to take in the crater from the lake. "There are daily boat tours," Brian described. "Not only do you get to see the walls of the volcano and the surrounding mountains, but you get to explore the lake itself. Most trips stop at Wizard Island, which is a world of its own. The geology is very young here, only seven thousand years old. It's amazingly refreshing to swim here, though it's cold—fifty degrees. There's a jumping rock, a fifteen-foot-drop to the lake's surface. There are times on the tour in Chaski Bay when you can see all the way to the bottom. The blue-green water makes you think of the Caribbean. You can fish in Crater Lake if you wish, and since the fish are nonnative, you can keep as many as you wish. Since the water is so pure, the fish taste exceptionally good. It's a seven-hundred-foot drop down to the lake, and you have to cover that elevation gain when you come back up."

There are two camping options within the park. Mazama Village Campground has two hundred wooded sites. "Mazama is best for people who'd prefer an easier camping experience," Brian continued. "You have restaurants and showers nearby, plus great evening programs for the family. Lost Creek is much smaller—just sixteen sites—and limited to tents. [Visitors should know that both campgrounds are a short drive from the rim.] Some people like to camp at nearby Diamond Lake, another beautiful patch of water about thirty minutes north, and make day trips to Crater Lake. You can take your boat (or rent one), and Diamond Lake has a resort with full amenities."

Anyone visiting Crater Lake should plan a stop at the regal Crater Lake Lodge, a structure dating back to 1915. The lobby and dining room, which look out upon the lake and surrounding peaks, feature logs with intact branches, which complement its Pacific Northwest surroundings.

BRIAN ETTLING has worked as a summer seasonal ranger at Crater Lake for the past twenty-two years. He is originally from St. Louis, Missouri. Upon graduating from William Jewell College in Kansas City, Missouri, in 1992, he took a cross-country train trip from Kansas City to Oregon for a summer job at Crater Lake. Crater Lake made such an impression on him that he has worked there during the summers ever since. Besides working at Crater Lake, he also spent sixteen winters working as a seasonal ranger in Everglades National Park, Florida. Since 2010, Brian spends his off-season trying to protect our national parks and natural world by teaching and public speaking on the problem of climate change and the things we can do to make this a healthier planet.

If You Go

▶ **Getting There:** The nearest commercial airport is in Medford, which is served by Horizon Air (800-547-9308; www.horizonair.com) and United Express (800-241-6522; www.united.com), among others.

▶ **Best Time to Visit:** Snow will sometimes linger around Crater Lake until late June and arrive in October, so July through September is your best bet.

▶ **Campgrounds:** Mazama Village Campground has sites for both tents and RVs. Half of the 200 sites can be reserved in advance (888-774-2728; www.craterlakelodges.com), with sites beginning at $21. The tent sites at Lost Creek are first come, first served; sites are $10. Sites at nearby Diamond Lake can be reserved through www.recreation.gov.

▶ **Activities:** Hiking, swimming, fishing, and biking.

DESTINATION

36

OWYHEE CANYONLANDS

RECOMMENDED BY **Kirk Richardson**

The arid and sparsely inhabited southeast corner of Oregon is a far cry from the mist-enshrouded Douglas firs and lush valleys lying west of the Cascades—the terrain most visitors equate with the Beaver State. Here, vertiginous canyons carved by the Owyhee River and veritable seas of sagebrush make up one of the Lower 48's wildest, most unspoiled regions—the Owyhee Canyonlands.

OPPOSITE:
The sun sets on the Owyhee River, a few miles downstream from Three Forks.

"The Owyhee region is largely unknown, but to me it's on the scale of the Grand Canyon," Kirk Richardson enthused. "The entire Owyhee Basin, which stretches into southwestern Idaho and northwestern Nevada, encompasses nine million acres. Over two million acres are managed as Wilderness Study Areas. [This is a step in the process of permanent wilderness designation.] There are so many outdoor recreation opportunities here—hiking, world-class rafting, bird watching, fishing, and my favorite pastime, rock climbing. There's abundant desert wildlife, innumerable archaeological sites, and even hot springs. From certain vantage points, you can get a clear line of sight across the northern reaches of the Great Basin to Steens Mountain."

The Owyhee Canyonlands of Oregon begin at the border of Nevada, Idaho, and Oregon and stretch north toward the small town of Adrian. The lifeblood of the region pulses from the four branches of the Owyhee River—the Main stem, North, South, and Middle. The four branches comprise more than two hundred miles of river flowing in a generally northern direction to its terminus with the Snake. In some places, walls of rhyolite climb a thousand feet from the river; in others, formations resemble oversize sand castles. The five million acres here are crisscrossed by a series of rough roads that lead to several primitive campgrounds that can be accessed by four-wheel-drive vehicles. One of these modest campgrounds is called Three Forks, situated at the spot where the North, Middle, and Main forks of the Owyhee come together, presided over by Three Forks Dome. "You have to really want to get there," Kirk continued, "as it's a thirty-plus-mile ride on dirt roads to reach the rim of the canyon, and then a very rough road down. But once you reach the river, there's good fishing for native redband trout, and you can explore the different river canyons on foot." At many spots along the river, you'll come upon white etchings on black basalt—petroglyphs. These geometric drawings, ranging from bird tracks to human figures to circles, are believed to have had spiritual meaning for the Northern Paiute, Bannock, and Shoshone tribes that once lived here. Three Forks is also home to one of Oregon's finest hot springs, several river crossings and a short hike from the camping area; in one of the pools, you can sit below a warm-water waterfall as the Owyhee flows below you. "One downside of camping at Three Forks is that there can be lots of rattlesnakes in the warmer weather," Kirk added. "If you get out of your tent in the night to answer nature's call, don't step on any moving sticks."

A second, somewhat more accessible, campground is Succor Creek, a jumping-off point for some fine hikes and rock-climbing opportunities. "Succor Creek is near Leslie Gulch," Kirk continued, "and hiking up Leslie gives you access to several other gulches, including Juniper, Runaway, Upper Leslie, and Dago. Dago has the most established climbing routes." Even if you're not a climber, you'll appreciate the spectacular rock formations around Leslie Gulch, and the nearby Honeycombs, a colorful series of pinnacles, cliffs, and towers. (The Juniper Gulch Trail is a great bet.) Succor Creek is a good place to hunt for thunder eggs (spherical geodes containing agates and other minerals), and is a prime spot to view a host of raptors, including golden eagles, ferruginous and red-tailed hawks, and peregrine falcons. Slocum Creek is perhaps the most accessible of the Owyhee's campgrounds. The drive in, which exposes impressive slot canyons and towering hoodoos, is worth the trip in itself. Slocum provides easy access to the hiking and bouldering opportunities in Leslie Gulch. It's also a great spot to scan the canyon walls for bighorn; it was here that the animals were reintroduced in the mid-1960s. During the mating season in early fall, rams will square off and butt horns. The concussion of these encounters bounces about the canyons like gunshots. Pronghorns call the Owyhee home, and herds of Rocky Mountain elk and mule deer migrate here to pass the winter. Early risers hiking the sagebrush steppe of the canyonlands in the spring may come upon greater sage-grouse on their leks (mating grounds), where males engage in complex courtship dances. (While not officially on the endangered-species list, the sage-grouse's future is very uncertain; the Owyhee is certainly a stronghold of the species.)

Note: The Owyhee Canyonlands hold many treasures, but require preparation and a certain level of self-reliance, as there are no amenities once you leave asphalt. Make sure your gas tank is full and carry extra gas, a full-size spare, and lots of water. Travel on some roads—particularly into Three Forks—is strongly discouraged after rain.

"I'm passionate about conservation, and a few years ago, I wanted to get involved beyond financially supporting such organizations," Kirk recalled. "I eventually got a seat on the board of the Oregon Natural Desert Association. The biggest preservation project we're working on is in the Owyhee Canyonlands. One of the really great things about the Owyhee is that it has resisted conquest for nearly two hundred years, ever since it was first discovered by Europeans. Nobody—the Hudson's Bay Company, the U.S. military— could 'de-wildify' it. Now we have a chance to save it for future generations. Preserving something on the scale of the Owyhee Canyonlands—two million acres of wilderness, the largest conservation opportunity in the Lower 48 states—would be a game changer in this part of the world."

KIRK RICHARDSON works for KEEN Footwear on corporate responsibility in Portland, Oregon.

If You Go

► **Getting There:** The camping spots described here are a two- to four-hour drive from Boise, Idaho, which is served by many carriers. Visitors will be best served with a four-wheel-drive vehicle with reasonably high clearance. Wild Owyhee (www.wildowyhee.org) provides detailed directions to each campground and sites of interest.

► **Best Time to Visit:** Late spring through fall. Do note that daytime temperatures in the summer will be quite warm.

► **Campgrounds:** There are four primitive campgrounds within Oregon's Owyhee Canyonlands: Three Forks, Succor Creek, Slocum Creek, and Anderson Crossing (the most remote). These campgrounds offer few amenities beyond pit toilets.

► **Activities:** Wildlife viewing, hiking, rock climbing, fishing, rock hunting, rafting.

DESTINATION

37

NORTH COAST

RECOMMENDED BY **Chris Emerick**

In 1967, Governor Tom McCall signed the Oregon Beach Bill, giving Oregonians (and visitors) "free and uninterrupted use of the beaches" along the state's more than four hundred miles of coastline. Each section of the coast—from the California border to the mouth of the mighty Columbia—has its charms. For Chris Emerick, the majestic temperate rain forests, rugged coastline replete with numerous sea stacks, and inviting resort towns —as well as opportunities for first-rate kiteboarding—make the north coast especially inviting. "You have a host of classic Oregon experiences available on the stretch of coast from the town of Manzanita in the north to Lincoln City in the south," he shared. "You can paddle a kayak in the ocean or on one of the rivers that flow into the Pacific, hike, harvest clams or crabs, fish, and surf. And there are a number of fine campgrounds to choose from. The summer gets the majority of the coast's visitors. I especially love to get out there in the off-season."

Chris's off-season camping adventures are facilitated by the use of a camper van.

"The camper van makes it possible to be comfortable when traditional tent camping would be unpleasant at best," he continued. "I like to describe it as somewhere in between sleeping on the ground and a glamping experience with four-hundred-thread-count sheets and champagne. Pop-up campers offer easily accessible beds, petite kitchens, and fold-down tables for eating. You don't have to cook in the rain. If I'm out kiteboarding, I don't have to change into my wetsuit on the side of the road . . . or more importantly, I don't have to change out of it in the cold and rain. I can step inside, turn on the propane heater, and be cozy. I like to call it 'vamping.' The camper vans are compact enough that they're much easier to drive and park than an RV and more economical. You can set up in the car-camping section of most campgrounds. I've been a van camper for a long time,

OPPOSITE:

Oregon's north coast offers abundant water activities . . . and the Eurovan provides a dry sanctuary from the occasional rain.

DESTINATION

38

NORRFÄLLSVIKEN

RECOMMENDED BY **Eva Svärd**

Citizens of Sweden enjoy one of the world's most generous nationally mandated vacation policies: twenty paid vacation days from their employer and sixteen paid national holidays. In the summertime, many Swedes like to enjoy their abundant leisure time camping. "Camping's popularity dates back to the 1930s, when the government made it law that people should have vacations," began Eva Svärd. "At that time, they began developing camping sites; people would travel to them by bike, carrying their tent. Camping really took off around 1970; now there are nearly a thousand campgrounds around Sweden, most of them near the sea or a lake. Visitors from Germany and Holland seem to like the lakes, whereas the Swedes like the coast."

And one area of Sweden's 2,000-mile coastline that's becoming increasingly popular as a camping spot is Höga Kusten, or the High Coast, which sits along the nation's northeastern edge on the Gulf of Bothnia in Västernorrland County. The High Coast takes its name not from towering mountains, but from the fact that the land here has risen significantly—more than 2,500 feet—since the last Ice Age. (Scientists believe that the land has risen as a result of melting glaciers, which acted as a balance weight of sorts. As the weight of the glaciers decreased, the land rose . . . and continues to rise.) The landscape here is characterized by steep granite cliffs and bright-blue Baltic waters. A favorite camping spot along the High Coast is Norrfällsviken.

"Norrfällsviken was once a fishing village," Eva continued, "and dates back more than three hundred and fifty years. There's no longer any commercial fishing here, but many people come in the summertime for vacation. Many of the old fishermen's homes—all neatly painted in red—are now summer cottages. The campground at Norrfällsviken is nicely situated near the sea. Open your door and you're right on the water."

OPPOSITE: Norrfällsviken combines comfortable camping with the charm of an old High Coast fishing village.

DESTINATION

40

179

In Sweden, camping takes on a somewhat different connotation than it does for many in North America. Some campgrounds more resemble resorts than the bare-bones facilities common on U.S. Forest Service holdings. And tent dwellers make up a minute proportion of the camping populace; according to a survey conducted in 2013 by the trade group Camping Sweden, 71 percent opt for caravans (that is, pull-behind self-contained campers), 15 percent opt for cottages; 8 percent choose motor homes, and 6 percent select tents. Though Swedish-style camping may be a bit less rustic than Americans might be used to, it is certainly popular—during the summer, more Swedes stay at campgrounds than in hotels or youth hostels. "For Swedes, the caravan is like a home away from home," Eva added. "People may take their caravan to a campground and stay all summer. People use them like a summer cottage." (Interestingly, there is a concept in Sweden called *allemansrätt*—every man's right—which allows people to enjoy the Swedish countryside and pitch a tent pretty much wherever they choose . . . even if it happens to be on private property. As long as you're not on farmland, not in sight of any house, and limit your stay to a night or two, you're good to go. You're also free to forage wild mushrooms and berries. Anything you bring into the wild, of course, should leave with you.)

By most standards, Norrfällsviken would fall into the resort category of campground. Not only are there hookups available for your caravan or RV, but also cable and satellite TV and Wi-Fi. There is a restaurant on-site and another in the nearby village; fresh bread can be delivered each morning to your campsite. If your children are along, there's a petting zoo, regular films, and other hosted activities. You can swim in the pool, swim in the cool Baltic, play tennis, play mini golf (or full-size golf at a nearby course), or rent a bicycle to get in a ride or a boat to explore the calm waters of the surrounding archipelago. You can conclude your busy day with a dip in one of the hot tubs near the marina or a sit in the campground's wood-fired sauna—this is Sweden, after all! Whether you're in a caravan or a motor home or a tent, you'll likely find your neighbors grilling their dinner— according to Eva, barbecuing is an intrinsic part of the Swedish camping tradition.

Swedes are passionate boaters, and sailing is a beloved pastime. While camping in Norrfällsviken, you'll want to take time to get out on the water. If you're not game to take a boat out yourself, consider boarding a regularly scheduled excursion to the island of Ulvön . . . but be prepared for the uniquely Swedish phenomenon of *surströmming*, or fermented herring. Fisherman have plied the waters around Ulvön since the sixteenth century for Baltic herring. The fishing season in this part of Sweden has always been short, and in the days before refrigeration, fermentation proved an economical method for preserving fish for year-round consumption. The third Thursday in August marks *Ulvöregattan*, or Ulvön Day, and the official decanting of the swelled tin cans of herring. The aroma is, at best, well . . . pungent. "It smells like Hell when they begin opening the tins, but the taste is much better than the smell," Eva described, "though it's still an acquired taste. It's usually served with flatbread, potato slices, and cheese. You roll the bread with the other ingredients to make a sandwich."

Some may feel the need for a burst of fresh air after the olfactory experience of *surströmming*. A hike up *Skuleberget* (Skule Mountain) should do the trick. Many Swedes consider the ascent of Skule Mountain a compulsory activity when visiting the High Coast. The trail takes you through thick pine forests and climbs toward vistas revealing surrounding mountains and islands dotting the Baltic. The top of Skule Mountain is the highest point resulting from the glacial uplift. You can enjoy a snack or lunch at the Top Cabin restaurant before heading down.

A serving of *surströmming* is optional.

EVA SVÄRD is marketing manager at SCR Swedish Camping, the National Swedish Campsite Association, which represents approximately 450 campsites across the country.

If You Go

▶ **Getting There:** Örnsköldsvik Airport is convenient to Norrfällsviken and the High Coast and has regular service from Stockholm via NextJet (+46 771 90 00 90; www.nextjet.se/sv).

▶ **Best Time to Visit:** The campground at Norrfällsvikens is open May through October, though the best weather arrives in July and August.

▶ **Campgrounds:** Norrfällsvikens Camping & Stugby (+46 0613 213 82; www.camping.se) is situated near the heart of the High Coast and has extensive amenities including beach, pool, playground, restaurant, cable and satellite TV, convenience store, sauna, hot tubs, and Wi-Fi. Sites start at 195 Swedish kronor (roughly $25 USD).

▶ **Activities:** Swimming, boating, hiking, golf, tennis, sightseeing.

DESTINATION

40

AROLLA

RECOMMENDED BY **Laurence and Georges Reif**

Mountaineers and day hikers alike have long been drawn to the spires and valleys of the Swiss Alps. And there's no base camp that gets you closer than Camping Arolla—Europe's highest campground.

"My wife and I have long been going to Switzerland from our home in France to climb," Georges Reif observed. "The high valleys make the peaks very accessible. Places like Chamonix and Zermatt can be a bit crowded. They're really ski resorts more than hiking destinations. About fifteen years ago, we discovered Arolla. There is a small ski resort there, but it's really more given over to alpinism and hiking. The campground here rests at almost two thousand meters, and it's the beginning point of many different trails. Every day, you can do a different hike."

Arolla is a small hamlet in the Swiss canton of Valais, which rests at the southern end of Val d'Hérens, an unspoiled valley along Switzerland's border with France and Italy. The valley is flanked by two mountain peaks of more than 13,123 feet, Dent Blanche and Dent d'Hérens; the vistas here scream "Switzerland tourism poster." Many mountains rise above Arolla, most notably Mont Collon and Pigne d'Arolla, just under and over 12,000 feet, respectively. This region of the Pennine Alps first came to international attention in 1865, when British mountaineer Edward Whymper first summited the nearby Matterhorn, which rises 9,000 feet directly above Zermatt. This was the climax of what some call the "golden age" of mountaineering, an interest in alpinism that was reflected in the growth and prominence of the Alpine Club in London. (Regrettably, four of Whymper's fellow Alpine Club members fell to their deaths during the descent.) While the peaks around Arolla have not gained as much notoriety as Mont Blanc to the west in Chamonix and the Matterhorn in Zermatt to the east, it lies along the course of the Haute Trail, the famed

OPPOSITE:
Arolla is
the highest
campground
in Europe,
resting at nearly
6,500 feet.
Pigne d'Arolla, in
the background,
is 12,450 feet.

DESTINATION

41

hiking/backcountry-skiing path that connects the two mountains. "We have many visitors in Arolla who are hiking the Haute Trail," Georges continued. "People who are doing the hike [which can take anywhere from eight to fourteen days] like to stop because we have showers and washing machines. It's a chance to prepare for the remaining hike." (Other amenities at Camping Arolla include an on-premises store where fresh bread is delivered each day at eight a.m., as well as a restaurant/pizzeria five minutes away.)

Arolla attracts both visitors who stay in camper vans and those who pitch a tent. "The camper van guests tend to stay for shorter periods, and they seem to come to enjoy the wonderful scenery," Georges observed. "The tent campers tend to stay much longer—from ten days to three or four weeks. They are here to walk or climb, and use Arolla as a base camp." There are dozens of day hikes that begin at or near Arolla, walks that appeal to hikers with a broad range of abilities. "If you want to get out on a glacier, there are nice flat walks that would be easy for people who are in moderately good shape," Georges added. "There are other more technical and strenuous climbs for experienced mountaineers." When pressed to choose a favorite, Georges paused and eventually named Pas de Chèvre. Roughly six miles in length, the Pas de Chèvre trail leads hikers from the pastoral Val d'Hérens to the icy environs of the Cheilon Glacier . . . and back down. To reach the high point of the trail at the Pas de Chèvre, you'll need to climb a series of ladders, known as *via ferrata* ("iron road" in Italian). Via ferrata provide a series of rungs, rails, and cables that permit hikers lacking technical rock-climbing experience to scale rock faces that would otherwise be beyond their skill. The Pas de Chèvre is an exhilarating hike (reaching an altitude of almost 9,400 feet), but the vistas from the summit of the pass—including the Matterhorn, the Weisshorn, and Mont Blanc de Cheilon—are more than commensurate with the effort involved. "We attract many different kinds of mountain people to Arolla," Georges added. "Less-experienced hikers will often meet more-experienced alpinists who will take them along on more-difficult hikes and show them how to get along." As you make your way through the mountains, you may spot chamois, a member of the goat/antelope family, springing from rock to rock.

For those who've graduated to mountain climbing, Arolla is equally well situated. "There are six big mountain huts accessible from the campground," Georges explained. "People who hope to reach the summits of the neighboring mountains can hike up to the hut, stay overnight, and then complete their climb the following day and either stay in the hut on the way down or return to the campground. If visitors aren't ready to climb on their own, there are mountain guides who can work with you. Climbing courses are also available."

Beyond the hiking challenges and scenic wonders of Val d'Hérens, a visit to Arolla affords you a chance to partake in a bit of Swiss culture. In the nearby town of Evolène, you can sample local dairy specialties like Raclette du Valais, a cow's-milk cheese that's served by warming the cheese round by a fire and then scraping the melted cheese onto a plate. Raclette is usually served with gherkins, onions, rye bread, and ham. (Fondue is also available, of course.) Another special tradition in Val d'Hérens that you might wish to observe is cow fighting. The region is home to the Hérens breed of cows, which naturally fight each other to gain dominance over the herd. Their feisty behavior is especially in evidence in June, when the animals move to mountain pastures; during this time, festivals are organized where the cows will square off to determine which animal will become *La Reine des Reines*—that is, "Queen of the Queens." (These are not fights to the death; the cows' horns are blunted, and the battles are mostly shoving matches.)

LAURENCE AND GEORGES REIF have been campers and mountaineers for more than thirty years. They enjoy hiking, climbing, alpinism, and ski touring. Before acquiring Camping Arolla in 2014, Laurence and Georges managed a campsite and a mountain hut in France.

If You Go

▶ **Getting There:** Geneva is the nearest large airport to Arolla (roughly two and a half hours) and is served by most major international carriers.

▶ **Best Time to Visit:** Camping Arolla is open from mid-June through mid-September.

▶ **Campgrounds:** Camping Arolla (+41 27 283 22 95; www.camping-arolla.com) has both tent and camper van sites with many amenities, including hot showers, washing machines, and Wi-Fi. A site for two campers will run approximately €20.

▶ **Activities:** Hiking, mountaineering.

DESTINATION

41

BIG BEND NATIONAL PARK

RECOMMENDED BY **David Elkowitz**

Deep in the heart of West Texas rests Big Bend National Park, a place that defies easy classification . . . but may very well make you reconsider the way you think about the Lone Star State.

"It's hard to characterize Big Bend," David Elkowitz began, "because there's such a diversity of habitats. As you drive in from the north entrance you begin to see the southern end of the Rocky Mountains in the U.S., peaks that reach almost eight thousand feet. An hour's drive to the south, you have the Rio Grande, separating Texas from Mexico. Through much of the park, you have desert habitat, with creosote bush, mesquite, and many varieties of cactus. A number of avian flight paths intersect here, so there's excellent birding, including many rare species passing through. There's also a diversity of wildlife that ranges from black bear to javelina (which resemble smallish wild boars, though are a quite distinct species) to mountain lion. There are a number of fine day hikes and backcountry overnight hikes, even the chance to combine off-road driving or river rafting with backcountry exploration. If there's a unifying element to the many sides of Big Bend, I'd say it's that they're all wild, remote, and beautiful."

"Everything's bigger in Texas," as the old saw goes, and this aphorism certainly speaks to the grand, open spaces of Big Bend. The park encompasses more than 800,000 acres, extending north from the point where the Rio Grande turns to the northeast before its long, meandering southeastern course to the Gulf of Mexico; the turn is the "big bend." One hundred eighteen miles of the river flow along the southern boundary of the park. The riparian zone along the Rio Grande provides critical habitats for a variety of plant and animal life. Much of the midsection of the park is given over to desert; in fact, Big Bend encompasses the largest protected swath of the Chihuahuan Desert in the United States.

OPPOSITE:
Big Bend
National Park
blends expansive
desert terrain
with rugged
mountains
you might not
expect in Texas.

DESTINATION

42

The Chisos Mountains dominate the northern side of the park, rising abruptly, some five thousand feet from the desert. Thanks to their elevation, the Chisos attract a bit more moisture than the surrounding environs and support different flora than is found in other parts of the park, including aspen, Arizona cypress, ponderosa pine, and madrone. The elevation also makes for cooler temperatures, and the Chisos region attracts many of Big Bend's bipedal visitors who are leery of the desert heat.

Most national parks, by their very nature, are a bit off the grid. Perhaps no park in the Lower 48 is further afield than Big Bend—the nearest airport with commercial flights is in Midland/Odessa, 235 miles to the northeast. Most visitors who make the effort to come this far stay for a while, and there are plenty of activities to make the trip worthwhile. "We have two hundred miles of established, well-cared-for trails," Dave continued, "from modest hikes well-suited for families to several rigorous multiday walks." A few of Dave's favorite day hikes are the Lost Mine, Window, Mule Ears Spring, and South Rim Trails. "For the modest amount of effort it takes (4.8 miles round-trip), Lost Mine (in the Chisos) gives you a tremendous view out over the park into Mexico—and the first southern vantage point is only a mile up the trail! The Window Trail, also in the Chisos, showcases a little more variety in terms of ecosystems. It starts in high country, going through scrub vegetation with great mountain views, and slowly drops down into a shady canyon. At the bottom of the trail is the window, a slot in the canyon where there's a steep drop-off; the whole Chisos Basin drains through here. Javelina, gray fox, and bear are sometimes seen on this trail. Mule Ears Spring (on the west side of the park) brings you across several arroyos to the spring, which looks like a Japanese garden against the dry surroundings. The 'mule ears' are a pair of peaks behind the spring that lead you to this little oasis."

There are three campgrounds operated by the park service in Big Bend: Rio Grande, Chisos Basin, and Cottonwood. Dave described the benefits of each: "Rio Grande is in the south part of the park and is well screened for tent campers by a large grove of cottonwoods. It's very popular in wintertime, and thanks to the proximity of the river, there's great birding. Chisos Basin is more popular in the summer, as it's cooler (temperatures in the eighties), being at an elevation of fifty-four hundred feet. Cottonwood is on the west side of the park in the desert. It's smaller and quieter, like a little oasis. Big Bend also offers a different kind of camping option—one hundred sixteen backcountry sites that you can drive into. Some you can reach with a car, some with a two-wheel-drive pickup, some require a four-wheel-drive. You have to bring everything you need along (including water) and take it back out, but you're pretty certain of having solitude."

Many park visitors will carve out a day (or more) to see Big Bend's dramatic canyons—some 1,500 feet deep—from the Rio Grande. "There are a number of day trips that can be done if the water is high enough, and a number of guide services have concessions to lead trips along the river," Dave explained. "Most sections of the river are very calm, though if you float the Santa Elena Canyon, there is a Class IV rapid that's best done with a guide or by experienced paddlers. One way to see some of the canyon without white water is to do what we call a 'boomerang' trip. You put in your raft or kayak at the Santa Elena Canyon trailhead and paddle upstream a few miles to Fern Canyon, then float back down with the current. In my opinion, no visit to the park is complete without some time on the river."

DAVID ELKOWITZ is the chief of interpretation (chief naturalist) at Big Bend National Park. He has been a National Park Service ranger since 1985, during which time he has served at six national parks, including southwestern parks such as Carlsbad Caverns, El Malpais, and Padre Island National Seashore. David is a graduate of the University of Connecticut with a BS in wildlife biology. He is a lifelong naturalist with special interest in ornithology and herpetology.

If You Go

▶ **Getting There:** The airport nearest Big Bend is in Midland/Odessa (235 miles from park headquarters), and is served by Continental Airlines (800-523-3273; www.continental.com) and American Airlines (800-433-7300; www.aa.com).

▶ **Best Time to Visit:** Big Bend sees most of its visitors in the winter and early spring. The park is open in the summer, and Dave recommends this as a great time to come if you stay in the Chisos, where it's cooler.

▶ **Campgrounds:** There are three park-service campgrounds in Big Bend: Rio Grande Village (one hundred sites), Chisos Basin (sixty sites), and Cottonwood (twenty-four sites). Basic amenities (but no hookups) are available; sites are $14/night. Limited reservations are available through Recreation.gov (877-444-6777). A privately run RV campground with hookups is available at Rio Grande Village (877-386-4383).

▶ **Activities:** Hiking, bird watching, paddling, scenic drives/four-wheel drives, fishing.

DESTINATION

42

UMPHANG WILDLIFE SANCTUARY

RECOMMENDED BY **Chris Clifford**

Whether it's the bountiful release of air-cleansing negative ions, the crashing roar of thundering columns of water, or the visual splendor of those columns sparkling in the sun, humans have long been drawn to waterfalls. In Thailand, the waterfall that stands above all others is Thi Lo Su, in the province of Tak.

"When Thai people travel, they tend to stay in Thailand," began Chris Clifford. "And when they're looking for a chance to experience cold weather—cold in this case being twenty degrees Celsius—they come north to Chiang Mai and the surrounding region. While the area immediately around Chiang Mai has become more developed, parts of the province of Tak to the west are still isolated and thus less crowded. I'm a white-water kayaker, and I became acquainted with the area—including the Umphang Wildlife Sanctuary—scouting out rivers to run in the wet season. A few times, I even used elephants to shuttle my kayak. As I've gotten older and now have a family I do less kayaking, but I've discovered the camping possibilities of the region."

The Umphang district rests toward the southern tip of the Tak province in northern Thailand. It's bordered by Mae Wong and Khlong Lan National Parks to the east, the border with Myanmar (Burma) to the west, and the Thung Yai and Huay Kha Kaeng wildlife sanctuaries to the south. Its thick forests—a tapestry of evergreen and deciduous trees—are dotted with teak, bamboo, and ironwood and provide shelter for elephants, leopards, langurs, bears, tigers, tapirs, and a host of rare birds, including the elusive hornbill. Wild-animal encounters are always a roll of the dice, but the centerpiece of the Umphang experience—the Thi Lo Su waterfall—is a constant. A number of drops combine to give Thi Lo Su an elevation of more than 650 feet; its width is roughly a quarter mile. "The falls are about a mile from the camping area," Chris continued. "There's a

OPPOSITE:

Thi Lo Su is the most majestic of Thai waterfalls, attracting both domestic and international travelers.

DESTINATION

43

good path along a lovely little creek that leads to the main falls. You can hear the roar of the falls well before you see them. When you do come around the bluff to the falls, the colors at Thi Lo Su are tremendous. The water is a stunning turquoise, and it's framed by the green rain forest and the caramel-shaded schist. There are three main stages of the falls and huge pools at each level where you can swim. If you wish, you can climb up all the way to the top to the Mae Klong, the fall's source."

Buddhism, the primary faith of Thailand, stresses that the path is the goal. This is certainly a good way to approach an adventure to Umphang and Thi Lo Su. First, there's the hundred-mile road leading to the town of Umphang from Mae Sot, which has been dubbed the "Death Highway." Highway 1090 boasts more than 1,200 curves as it climbs through agricultural land into the mist-clad mountains, though its eerie sobriquet stems from clashes between soldiers and communist insurgents in the late 1970s when the road was being constructed. Travel is not fast on the Death Highway, but it does offer great vistas of the rain forest and exposure to the different people that call this hill country home. These include ethnic communities of Karen, Hmong, Lahu, Lisu, Akha, and Yao. Once you reach the town of Umphang, it's another seven miles to the entrance of the sanctuary, and fifteen miles to the sanctuary's headquarters and campground. The campground is near the sanctuary's administrative headquarters. "The campground rests in a grass field interspersed with rain forest trees," Chris described, "and while there's no electricity for caravans, there are centralized showers and toilets, plus a cooking area. There's a small store that has electricity, and you can charge your camera or laptop there. People from one of the nearby Karen villages will often come into camp to visit and sell food and handicrafts. When they visit, they might offer a glass of Lao Khao, a local rice whiskey."

Though more and more people are discovering the Umphang region, its thick forests still maintain a wilderness aura, as Chris learned firsthand. "For me, camping is an excuse to go out in the forest," he mused. "It serves as a kind of meditation. A few years back, I hiked into the forest near Thi Lo Su. I had my four Labrador Retrievers with me. It was a moonlit night, and at bedtime, I set myself up under a mosquito net with a tent fly over the netting. Sometime in the night, I was awoken by some heavy purring. I turned around, and three feet from my face there was a full-grown male black panther. I was looking straight into its big emerald eyes, all very visible in the moonlight. I'd spent ten years in northern Australia working around big crocodiles and tended to be fairly calm around big wild animals. So I started speaking to the cat. I said, 'I'm not going to stay here, I'm just passing through.' Then the cat started pacing back and forth along the tent, the way you see big cats pace at the zoo. At one point it pawed the tent fly, and I pushed it away with my pillow. In retrospect, I think it was just hungry. Eventually it moved away from the tent to the base of a tree and sat down. It sat there for an hour, and I kept talking to it. Then it moved off. I had no idea where my dogs were the whole time. They must have smelled the cat and slipped away."

CHRIS CLIFFORD is field coordinator with the Border Consortium, which has been working with refugees who fled conflict in Burma/Myanmar since 1984 to provide food, shelter, and other forms of support in camps in western Thailand. Chris was previously land and sea management coordinator at Lockhart River Aboriginal Community for ten years, where he also completed his PhD in community-based planning. Originally from Narrabeen Beach in Sydney, Australia, Chris has always been enthusiastic about all water sports, particularly snorkeling, fishing, and surfing. During his university years, he became more interested in ecology and wilderness experiences, including outdoor activities such as bushwalking, camping, and white-water kayaking. Later, working with Aborigines on the remote Cape York Peninsula, he became more interested in understanding wilderness from a cross-cultural perspective.

If You Go

▶ **Getting There:** Umphang Wildlife Sanctuary is roughly seven hours from Chiang Mai by car, nine hours from Bangkok. Flights are available from Bangkok to Mae Sot (which is roughly four hours from Umphang) via Nok Air (www.nokair.com) and Solar Air (www.solarair.co.th).
▶ **Best Time to Visit:** The dry season—from October to mid-March—is the best time to visit northern Thailand.
▶ **Campgrounds:** Camping is available on the grounds of the Umphang Wildlife Sanctuary headquarters. Toilets and showers are available.
▶ **Activities:** Hiking, swimming, rafting, elephant riding, cultural sightseeing.

DESTINATION

43

BRYCE CANYON NATIONAL PARK

RECOMMENDED BY **Christopher Martens**

"Camping has been part of my life since I was very young," Christopher Martens recalled. "When I was twelve, I was on the Appalachian Trail for a week, and it set the mood for my career. In my early twenties, I drove from Florida to Alaska, camping the entire way—that was seventeen thousand miles! I've staked a tent in lots of places, but one camping experience that stands out is a trip I took with my family to Bryce Canyon National Park in Utah."

Bryce Canyon National Park sits near the bottom of southwestern Utah, about 140 miles northeast of the town of St. George, or 80 miles northeast of Zion National Park. At 56 square miles, Bryce is diminutive by western national park standards; Grand Canyon National Park, not far to the southwest as the crow flies, tops out at more than 1,900 square miles. But Bryce packs an incredible punch in its modest space. Much of the park is taken over with a series of 14 horseshoe-shaped "amphitheaters." (Canyon is a misnomer, as these large hollowed-out areas were created by a long geological history of sedimentation and erosion from rain, not from the force of a river.) The amphitheaters are populated with bizarre limestone formations that create an otherworldly landscape of slot canyons, arches, and spires called hoodoos. The hoodoos, a result of both frost-wedging (freeze/thaw cycles that creates cracks in the rocks) and eons of rain, take on a veritable Rorschach test of shapes—some look like people, some animals, one is even identified as E.T.! A blaze of colors and contours, the hoodoos are frequently bunched together to create mazes of wonderment.

Though Fremont and Anasazi people spent time in the Bryce Canyon area from 200 to 1200 AD, it was the Paiute Indians that occupied the region for much of the second half of the twentieth century. The Paiutes, incidentally, have a slightly different explana-

OPPOSITE:

The limestone formations at Bryce Canyon create an otherworldly landscape amidst the deserts of southern Utah.

DESTINATION

44

tion for Bryce's geologic wonders, as shared by a Paiute elder named Indian Dick to a naturalist in 1936:

> Before there were any Indians, the Legend People, To-when-an-ung-wa, lived in that place. There were many of them. They were of many kinds—birds, animals, lizards and such things, but they looked like people. They were not people. They had power to make themselves look that way. For some reason the Legend People in that place were bad; they did something that was not good, perhaps a fight, perhaps some stole something . . . the tale is not clear at this point. Because they were bad, Coyote turned them all into rocks. You can see them in that place now all turned into rocks; some standing in rows, some sitting down, some holding on to others. You can see their faces, with paint on them just as they were before they became rocks. The name of that place is Angka-ku-wass-a-wits (red painted faces).

It was John Wesley Powell—the one-armed adventurer who first floated the Colorado through the Grand Canyon—and Captain Clarence Dutton who brought the existence of Bryce to the outside world . . . though it was a Mormon emissary named Ebenezer Bryce who would displace the Paiutes and create a small settlement. Bryce and his family eventually moved on to northern Arizona, but the name stuck. Bryce was originally to be known as Utah National Park, but in 1928, the park was renamed Bryce Canyon.

"My family and I were doing the southwest park circuit," Christopher continued. "We'd flown into Las Vegas and spent a few days, and then headed to the Grand Canyon, then on to Bryce, and finally to Zion. At each park, we were trying to find the coolest campsite, and at Bryce, we thought we'd found a pretty good one. We had to hike our stuff up a little ways, but the site looked out over the campground. My family was setting all the gear up as I jumped in the car to run to the store. When I got back a few minutes later, my kids came running down. 'Dad, you've gotta see this.' I followed them up a small trail behind the campsite, up a slight hill. There, at the top of the hill, we were on the edge of Bryce Amphitheater, looking east at all the spires, over the whole canyon. The look of wonder on their faces was unforgettable. It was like we'd found a national park in our backyard . . . which we had!"

Bryce boasts two campgrounds, North and Sunset. Both are located a short distance from the visitor center, the Bryce Canyon Lodge, a general store, and the Bryce Amphitheater, and both offer similar amenities—flush toilets, potable water, and pay showers/laundry nearby. Bryce sits at an elevation of eight thousand feet, and both camp-sites are greener than you might expect in these arid climes, shaded by ponderosa pines and dotted with summer wildflowers. (Though days can be warm in the summer, temps cool down nicely for comfortable sleeping.) Thanks to its elevation, isolation, and low humidity, Bryce boasts exceedingly good air quality; on a clear day from the highest points in the park, you can see more than one hundred miles. The air clarity and lack of light pollution make Bryce Canyon National Park one of North America's darkest spots and thus a premier stargazing locale; one can see some 7,500 stars with the naked eye here, whereas only 2,000 stars can be viewed in most places (far fewer in cities). The park's proximity to the heavens is celebrated each June with the Bryce Canyon Astronomy Festival.

As to the exact location of Christopher's killer campsite, you'll have to explore Bryce for yourself!

There are a number of ways to take in the park's geologic wonders. The most popular is to drive the park road to Rainbow Point, roughly eighteen miles. There are thirteen pullouts along the way, so you can take in different perspectives of the amphitheaters and their panoply of pinnacles. Horseback riding (through a concessionaire near Bryce Canyon Lodge) is another way to tour the park. If time permits, consider a hike that drops down into the Bryce Amphitheater so you can roam amongst the fanciful rock formations. The Queen's Garden Trail is gentle and takes you past Queens Castle and Queen Victoria. The Navajo Loop Trail is a bit steeper but perhaps even more dramatic. It takes you through "Wall Street" (a narrow slot between sheer cliffs) and provides grand views of Thor's Hammer, perhaps Bryce's most photographed formation, as well as the Silent City, a formation that resembles a cityscape.

CHRISTOPHER MARTENS is business director of camping for Johnson Outdoors, a global outdoor recreation equipment products company whose brands include Eureka!, Silva, Jetboil, and Old Town® canoes and kayaks. Before joining Johnson Outdoors, Christopher served as CEO of Respect Your Universe, business director and merchandise director at Nike, Inc., global business director of apparel for the 2008 Beijing Olympics, and divisional merchandise manager for Global Nike ACG and Global Nike Outerwear. He also spent eleven years at EMS (Eastern Mountain Sports) in a variety of positions, including product manager of tents, sleeping bags, and cooking (stoves, hydration, food, energy products).

If You Go

▶ **Getting There:** The nearest commercial airport to Bryce is in St. George, Utah (roughly 140 miles away), and is served by Delta (800-221-1212; www.delta.com) and United (800-864-8331; www.united.com). Las Vegas is the closest major airport (roughly 270 miles away).

▶ **Best Time to Visit:** Bryce is open year-round, though parts of the park are closed in the winter. July sees the warmest temperatures, but it cools down nicely at night. Mid-April through October should be snow-free.

▶ **Campgrounds:** There are two campgrounds in Bryce—North (99 sites) and Sunset (100 sites). Both are located near the visitor center and Bryce Amphitheater, and both have flush toilets and potable water. Limited RV spots (no hookups) and reserved sites are available; contact Recreation.gov (877-444-6777) to make a reservation. Tent sites are $15.

▶ **Activities:** Hiking, horseback riding, various naturalist/interpretive activities.

DESTINATION 44

DINOSAUR NATIONAL MONUMENT

RECOMMENDED BY **Dan Johnson**

If Dinosaur National Monument were to pen an advertising slogan, it might go something like this:

Come for the dinosaurs. Stay for the rafting and camping.

"I think the name of the monument is both a blessing and a curse," began Dan Johnson. "Lots of people come to see the dinosaurs. Of course, there are no dinosaurs. But you can see many fossils. And with 211,000 acres of terrain, there's much more beyond the dinosaur fossils for people to explore. There are two world-class rivers in the park—the Green and the Yampa—to explore. There are also a number of cultural sites, ranging from petroglyphs carved by the Native American people who used to call this canyon country home to old pioneer homesteads. A facet of Dinosaur that I appreciate is that it's not as developed as some parks. It's more rugged, cut through with backcountry roads that demand four-wheel drive. A visit here is a chance to step back into the history of the northern Colorado plateau. The land is little changed."

Dinosaur National Monument stretches from the northwest corner of Colorado west into Utah, a vast swatch of high-desert country. The monument encompasses hundreds of miles of river corridors with canyon walls reaching heights of more than two thousand feet, and rugged peaks eclipsing nine thousand feet. The first iteration of the monument came into being in 1915 a few years after a paleontologist named Earl Douglass came upon the fossil beds near the town of Vernal in the northeastern corner of Utah. The fossil beds—which would come to be known as Carnegie Quarry—held myriad specimens, including remnants of eight dinosaurs: *Allosaurus fragilis*, *Allosaurus jimmadseni*, *Apatosaurus*, *Barosaurus*, *Camarasaurus*, *Diplodocus*, *Dryosaurus*, and *Stegosaurus*. The

original eighty acres around the fossil beds were expanded to the monument's current dimensions in 1938.

For budding paleontologists—or lovers of the program *Dinosaur Train*—a visit to the Quarry Exhibit Hall (which sits above the actual quarry) is a must. "The Quarry Exhibit Hall is home to the Wall of Bones, where you'll find some fifteen hundred unexcavated fossils sticking out of the rock where it's eroded away," Dan described. "You're confronted with a rock wall that's full of recognizable bones—femurs, thighbones, jawbones. The first reaction is 'WOW!' In addition to the bones, you see multiple rock layers from different time periods—the time of dinosaurs, the time before the dinosaurs. You get to experience the size and scope of life on this planet and how it has changed with whatever's been thrown at it. It gives where we are now in history a clearer context." Visitors can even touch 149-million-year-old dinosaur fossils.

As mentioned above, visitors would be doing themselves a disservice by limiting their monument visit to an afternoon at the Quarry Exhibit Hall. Dan highlighted a few favorite activities. "A river trip gives you a very different perspective of how water and time have shaped this country. There are several concessionaires that run day trips on the Green in the Split Mountain Canyon area of the park. It gives guests a chance to sit back and enjoy the scenery while someone else does the work. You can also opt to do a multiday trip on the Green or Yampa. They're very different rivers. The Yampa flows through sandstone canyons and more-open country; the Green has more-pronounced canyons with darker rock. Most visitors don't get onto the rivers, but those who do leave changed, taken with the peacefulness of the place. To experience some of the monument's cultural attractions, pay a visit to view some of the petroglyphs (incised rock art) and pictographs (patterns painted on the rock) left by the Fremont people, who are believed to have lived in the area a thousand years ago. [Swelter Shelter and Cub Creek are two of the more easily accessible sites.] If you want to get a sense of the majesty and scope of this country, drive some of the scenic backcountry roads. The Harper's Corner, Island Park, and Echo Park Roads are all worthwhile."

Dinosaur offers a broad range of camping options. There are six campgrounds spread throughout the park. RVs are welcome in some, though there are no hookups and amenities are fairly basic (potable water, vault toilets, picnic tables, and fire rings). Dan described a few popular spots. "Green River is the closest campground to the Quarry Visitor Center. It's the biggest campground (seventy-nine sites) and is set along the banks of the river,

OPPOSITE:
A National Park Ranger offers dinosaur insights at the wall of bones at the Quarry Exhibit Hall.

DESTINATION

45

MOUNT RAINIER NATIONAL PARK

RECOMMENDED BY **Bill Gifford**

If you've ever flown into Seattle—or, for that matter, Portland or Vancouver—you've likely spied the massive stratovolcano that is Mount Rainier. Rising 14,410 feet above sea level, Rainier is the highest mountain in the Cascade Range and one of the most prominent peaks in the United States; it's also the most glaciated mountain in the Lower 48, with more than twenty-five major glaciers. Though more than fifty miles from downtown Seattle, on clear summer afternoons it feels as though you could reach out and touch its flanks from the Space Needle.

OPPOSITE: Monolithic Mount Rainier, as viewed from the Klapatche Park Trail.

Many will only admire Mount Rainier from afar. But visitors to Mount Rainier National Park can gain a greater appreciation of its volcanic roots, its glaciers, and its ancient forests.

"My family did a lot of camping as I was growing up, and my first visit to Mount Rainier was when I was about eight years old," Bill Gifford recalled. "We pitched our tent at Ohanapecosh. It was a great place for kids, with lots of big downed trees to climb around on. I remember hiking the trail along the Ohanapecosh River up to Silver Falls, crossing the river, and coming back—a five-mile loop. It made quite an impression on me. When I had a family of my own, I took them to Ohanapecosh Campground."

Mount Rainier National Park comprises some 370 square miles, with nearly all of its terrain designated as wilderness. Thirty-five square miles of the park are covered in snowfields and glaciers. Mount Rainier is America's fifth-oldest national park, protected for posterity in 1899. Mount Rainier rises quite abruptly from the surrounding Cascade Range, suggestive of its volcanic origins; the lowest point in the park has an elevation of 1,600 feet, the highest over 14,000 feet. Rainier is, in fact, considered an "episodically active" volcano, which means that the question is not if it will erupt, but when. The last

DESTINATION

47

recorded eruption was in the 1890s; according to the U.S. Geological Service, some 80,000 residents could be threatened should Rainier erupt, not to mention the impact on commerce and transportation. All of this is to say: a visit to Mount Rainier does pose a very modest risk. Should you accept the risk, one of the great rewards is a rich array of wildflowers. From mid-July to early September, you can expect vibrant displays of blue lupine, red paintbrush, pink daisies, yellow cinquefoil, pasque flower, elephant heads, and yellow glacier lilies . . . to name only a few.

Mount Rainier National Park has three drive-in campgrounds—White River (in the northeast section of the park) and Cougar Rock (in the southwest section), in addition to Ohanapecosh (in the southeast section). "All of the campgrounds are nicely developed, with flush-toilet restrooms and potable water," Bill continued. "And each is close to some wonderful hiking trails. I lead trips for Sierra Club here, and sometimes we'll use one of the campgrounds as a base and do a variety of day hikes." A favorite for Bill—and many others—is the Summerland Trail, which begins not far from White River Campground. "You start out in impressive old-growth forest," Bill described. "As you continue up along Fryingpan Creek, the trail eventually breaks out into gorgeous Summerland meadow, well above timberline. At this point, you're on the shoulder of the mountain, and you can take in glaciers above and the meadows below. In the earlier part of the summer, there are brilliant wildflower displays in the meadow. There are also many hoary marmots in the rocks. It's about four miles to the meadow. You can continue another mile up to Panhandle Gap, which sits at 6,800 feet." The panoramic vistas of Mount Rainier, plus the chance to spy mountain goats and herds of elk, make this fairly rigorous hike worthwhile.

Another day hike that Bill enjoys departs from a section of the park called Sunrise and leads up toward Skyscraper Pass and Skyscraper Mountain. "For much of the trail, you're out in the open, above timberline," Bill added. "The trail twists through meadows and past pretty streams, and there are great views from the ridgeline. You can go a little further to the top of Skyscraper Mountain (at an elevation of 7,078 feet). From here, you have panoramic views. To the east is the green cirque of Berkeley Park; to the north, the meadow of Grand Park; to the west is Winthrop Glacier; and to the south is Mount Rainier. I have to say that a special thing about Mount Rainier National Park is that there are really no bad choices when it comes to trails. All the options are good."

Those desirous of a bit more challenge might consider hiking the Wonderland Trail, which is ninety-three miles in length and circles Mount Rainier . . . or climbing to the summit. The former is generally done over ten days and entails 22,000 feet of elevation gain; the latter, while daunting, is in the realm of possibility for unseasoned climbers who are in good shape. (Roughly half of the 10,000 people that attempt to climb Rainier each year find success.) If you prefer to test your endurance on two wheels, consider the RAMROD (Ride Around Mount Rainier in One Day), where cyclists attempt to cover 154 miles (and 10,000 feet of elevation gain) on one July day.

Not all of Mount Rainier's wonders need be taken in on foot. One of the park's most memorable vistas of Mount Rainier and Emmons Glacier (Rainier's largest glacier) is found on clear days at Sunrise, the highest point (6,400 feet) in the park that you can reach by car. Another must-visit spot is Paradise, which boasts tremendous mountain views amidst a sea of wildflowers. It's also the site of the Paradise Inn, a classic lodge dating back to 1919.

BILL GIFFORD has been leading Sierra Club backpack trips in the Northwest since 1976, including trips to Mount Hood, Mount Rainier, Eagle Cap, Hells Canyon, the North Cascades, the Sky Lakes, Glacier Peak, the Three Sisters, and the Strawberry Mountains. Trees and wildflowers are his particular areas of expertise.

If You Go

▶ **Getting There:** Mount Rainier National Park is roughly fifty miles southeast of the Sea–Tac Airport, which is served by most major carriers.

▶ **Best Time to Visit:** Cougar Rock and Ohanapecosh Campgrounds are open from late May to late September; the White River and Mowich Lake (a hike-in campground) are open from late June through early October.

▶ **Campgrounds:** Cougar Rock, Ohanapecosh, and White River Campgrounds have a total of 480 campsites. No hookups or showers are available, though campgrounds have potable water, flush toilets, and fire grates. Some first-come, first-served sites are available, though you'd do best to make a reservation through Recreation.gov (877- 444-6777). Sites run $12 to $15.

▶ **Activities:** Hiking, biking, wildflower viewing.

DESTINATION

47

OLYMPIC NATIONAL PARK

RECOMMENDED BY **Rainey McKenna**

Olympic National Park rests on the northwestern edge of the continental United States, on a wind-and-rain-swept peninsula that's a study in gray, green, and, occasionally, blue. It could be said that Olympic National Park is three parks in one. First, it's a park for arboreal resources. The river valleys of the park have a remnant of what was once the greatest temperate rain forest in the world. Olympic National Park also boasts the largest coastal wilderness in the Lower 48—more than seventy miles of coastline, with very limited access points. Toward the eastern side of the park, there's wonderful high country. Despite its modest elevation (the highest peak in the Olympic range, Mount Olympus, tops out at 7,829 feet), the Olympics are home to a number of glaciers.

"Many people who come to Olympic National Park are amazed by the size of it," began Rainey McKenna. "There are some national parks you can see in one day—or at least get a sense of them. Olympic is a park that is very hard to see and experience in just one day. There are no roads that cut through the middle of the park; to see the coast, the rain forest, and the mountains in one day, you'd have to drive a minimum of five hours. The road system is like a wheel with spokes, each spoke accessing a different area of the park. If you want to really experience Olympic National Park, you should plan to visit for at least a couple of days . . . better yet, come for a week.

If there's a defining feature of Olympic National Park, it is water: the 135 inches of rain that fall on average in the Hoh River basin, and the more than 50 feet of snow that accumulates on Mount Olympus; the 4,000 miles of rivers and creeks that radiate from the park's central mountains, hosting healthy runs of salmon and steelhead and acting as a circulatory system for the park's varied ecosystems; and finally, the Pacific, which delivers the massive weather fronts to the Olympic Peninsula in the first place. The most celebrated

OPPOSITE:
Water, like
the Sol Duc
Waterfall, is the
defining feature
of Olympic
National Park.

DESTINATION

48

beneficiaries of all this water are the rain forests, and a hike up any of the river valleys on the west side of the park—the Quinault, Queets, Hoh, and Bogachiel—will likely redefine your idea of a "big tree." Sitka spruce and western hemlock dominate the landscape, but western red cedar, Douglas fir, and Engelmann spruce, among other conifers, are also present. Some of the largest specimens can approach 50 or 60 feet in circumference and reach heights of more than 200 feet. Almost as impressive are the mosses, ferns, and lichens that spring from the trunks of these giants. Even in the less-than-bright light that's the norm most of the year, the tangle of greens on display are so varied that they'd make the color-namers at Sherwin-Williams jump for joy. (Wandering through the rain forests, be on the lookout for Roosevelt elk, the largest of elk species.)

Olympic National Park's wonderfully diverse ecosystems provide a perfect palette for a host of outdoor adventures. "Given that so much of Olympic National Park is wilderness, and that we have more than six hundred miles of trails, hiking is certainly a popular activity," Rainey continued. "However, you don't have to be a hiker to experience the grandeur of the old-growth forests or the spectacularly rugged, beautiful, and wild coast. There are many short trails for easy day hikes, and most points of interest can be reached by car. The park is home to thirty-one native species of fish, including all five species of Pacific salmon and a number of trout. You can fish by boat or from shore on one of the park's many rivers or lakes. The park's two largest lakes, Lake Ozette and Lake Crescent, are also popular with boaters and kayakers. If you enjoy tide pooling, Olympic's tidal areas are some of the richest in North America. During the summer, rangers lead interpretive programs at beaches along the coast. If you go tide pooling, be aware of the tides and visit during low tide."

If you're looking for a more laid-back activity during your visit, there are several hot springs in the park, including those at the commercially operated Sol Duc Hot Springs Resort.

There are sixteen campgrounds spread throughout Olympic National Park, from the coast to the mountains. "Many of the campgrounds are open year-round—not necessarily with running water—though summer is by far the busiest time," Rainey explained. "Each campground offers a very different experience colored by the surrounding environment." At Hoh, you're deep in the rain forest along one of the park's great rivers. Heart O' the Hills is great for families and an ideal base camp to explore the camp. It's open year-round and is one of the park's largest campgrounds, with a hundred and five sites.

The Elwha campground rests in a beautiful valley, and you're close to the site of the Elwha River restoration project—the largest dam removal in U.S. history.

"With the Glines Canyon and Elwha Dams now gone, critical habitat-building sediment is once again moving downstream and salmon are migrating upstream to spawn for the first time in a hundred years," Rainey reflected. "It's amazing to see how the land and river are changing in the Elwha Valley, returning to what conditions were like before the dams. Everything in this ecosystem is tied to salmon and the nutrients they bring back from the sea. With the removal of the dams, return of the salmon, and the hard work of the park's restoration crews, vegetation is coming back and wildlife, such as deer, bears, and otters are returning to the areas that were once reservoirs. Visiting the Elwha now, you can see restoration and the web of life in action. It's a very dynamic environment."

RAINEY MCKENNA is a public information officer for Olympic National Park.

If You Go

▶ **Getting There:** The closest major airport is Sea–Tac, which is served by most major carriers; it's roughly three hours' drive to the park welcome center in Port Angeles by car. Kenmore Air (866-435-9524; www.kenmoreair.com) offers regular air-shuttle service from Seattle to Port Angeles.

▶ **Best Time to Visit:** Olympic National Park is situated in a temperate rain forest, and it can rain anytime. Nonetheless, July, August, and September are the driest months, with pleasant temperatures. Snow is generally gone from the high country by late June. The Olympic National Park website (www.nps.gov/olym) details backcountry guidelines and seasonal weather conditions.

▶ **Campgrounds:** There are sixteen campgrounds in Olympic National Park; all operate on a first-come, first-served basis, with the exception of Kalaloch Campground (reservations can be made here for the summer season at www.recreation.gov). You can learn more about each campground at the Olympic National Park website (www.nps.gov/olym). Sites range from $10 to $18.

▶ **Activities:** Hiking, tide pooling, wildlife viewing, fishing, swimming, kayaking, and boating.

DESTINATION

48

GRAND TETON NATIONAL PARK

RECOMMENDED BY **Jackie Skaggs**

Jackie Skaggs's first brush with Grand Teton National Park mirrors so many children's first national-park experience. It was from the backseat of the family sedan.

"I was born and raised in Pocatello, Idaho," Jackie began. "My family drove through the park when I was twelve years old, and I had my first camera, a Kodak Instamatic. I photographed the mountains, the bison, and the lingering snowdrifts during our family vacation to Grand Teton and Yellowstone. When I looked at those photos later, the Tetons absolutely burned into my consciousness on some primal level. Ten years later, when I graduated from college, my husband and I had to decide where to start our lives together. He said, 'We don't have to stay in Pocatello, you know. Where would you like to go?' I immediately thought of Jackson Hole and the Tetons. That was 1976. We managed to get seasonal jobs at Signal Mountain Lodge on the shores of Jackson Lake, and that was the beginning of an unrelenting obsession with this mysterious, magical place. Hook, line, and sinker, I was a goner."

The Tetons, just north of Jackson, Wyoming, are not America's tallest mountains, though they may be its most recognizable and photographed range of peaks. Rising abruptly from the valley floor, the distinctive jagged pinnacles of the compact Teton Range are iconic of the American West and the national park that bears its name. Grand Teton National Park encompasses 485 square miles, making up the southern sector of the vast Greater Yellowstone Ecosystem, the largest intact temperate ecosystem in the world. Forested hillsides slope down to the sage-covered valley floor and the banks of the shimmering Snake River, which runs north to south through the park. Beyond the river, the long, relatively flat valley unfolds. (The "hole" in Jackson Hole refers to the 55-mile-long, 13-mile-wide valley.) There are 250 miles of maintained hiking trails in the park,

OPPOSITE:

The Tetons, captured here after a late autumn snowfall, are America's most iconic mountain range.

ranging from gentle walks around Jenny Lake to the ambitious backcountry Teton Crest Trail. The Grand Teton, which measures 13,770 feet at its summit and rises some 7,000 feet from the valley floor, looms over it all. (Twelve other peaks in the Teton Range eclipse 12,000 feet in elevation.)

After thirty-eight years around the park—many of those in a public-affairs role, speaking to visitors each day—Jackie has a clear vision of Grand Teton's many appeals to campers. "I'd say there are four main reasons that visitors come to the park. First, it's the scenery, the awe-inspiring, in-your-face drama of the Teton peaks. The uplift is so abrupt from the sagebrush valley of Jackson Hole, it's overwhelming. This is accentuated by the range's proximity to the road. Whatever direction you approach the park from, the granite massifs are a breathtaking surprise. The Tetons provide the sort of vistas people equate with the big western parks.

"Wildlife is the second reason people come to GTNP. All the megafauna that people visit Yellowstone to see—bison, moose, elk, pronghorn, grizzly bears, and wolves—are here in Grand Teton too. The ecosystem has all the wildlife and flora that was present when the first Europeans arrived, another compelling reason to visit. Twenty years ago, you hardly ever heard of grizzly bear sightings in Grand Teton, but the population has expanded from Yellowstone and the bears have moved southward. Given that Grand Teton is only one-sixth the size of Yellowstone, you may even see grizzlies more frequently here. The fact that the bears are around makes the park feel a little wilder. You're a little more aware of making noise and likely to carry bear spray when you're out on the Teton trails. A third attraction is the range and variety of outdoor activities available throughout the park. The Tetons are one of the premier mountain climbing venues in the Lower 48. There are many routes that can be climbed, either by experienced climbers on their own with the help of a guidebook or by neophytes with the assistance of experienced guides. The Snake River, which flows through the middle of the park, is a great trout-fishing stream and provides a pristine setting for raft or kayak trips. Of course, there are many, many hikes. Thanks to the intimacy of GTNP, you can pack a bunch of activities into a day—say, a float trip in the morning, a hike in the afternoon, and a ranger program in the evening."

There are seven campgrounds in GTNP. A perennial favorite of tent campers is Jenny Lake. "You're situated very close to the base of the Tetons, so the vistas are especially dramatic," Jackie said. "It's a fairly small campground, only forty sites, and RVs aren't permitted. You have quick access to the central trail system, with hikes like String Lake, Cascade, and Paintbrush Canyon right from your tent. If you're looking for a mellower hike, there's the Jenny Lake Trail. I also like the Signal Mountain campground. There, you're close to boating and fishing on Jackson Lake, the largest glacial lake in the park. And, if you don't feel like fixing your meal, you can walk over to the Signal Mountain Lodge for a gourmet dinner or a hamburger. Wherever you camp, GTNP has features found in few other national parks. You can have a very rustic experience during the day, but then you can drive twenty or thirty minutes into Jackson and enjoy a more cultural experience, be it fine dining or attending a music festival or an art-exhibit opening. Then you can drive back and sleep under the stars. It's a unique balance, and I think it reflects what more people are looking for in a camping experience—roughing it, but with creature comforts."

Few people come away from the Grand Teton National Park unmoved. "There's a definite spiritual nature to the Tetons," Jackie opined. "It goes back to the native peoples. Many tribes came here in the summer [visiting tribes included Shoshone, Bannock, Blackfoot, Crow, Flathead, Gros Ventre, and Nez Perce] to hunt, but they also had a special reverence for the mountains that beaconed them. I feel it myself in a palpable, personal way. The Tetons have gotten me through some tough times, like the death of my father, who I was very close to. Whether it was watching the play of northern lights across an expansive night sky in November, skiing across the frozen surface of Jackson Lake in winter, seeing my first grizzly bear with newborn cubs, or just looking up at the soaring Teton peaks as I hiked and realizing just how small I felt in their shadow, the Tetons' permanence—seemingly unchangeable qualities—helped me heal many times, but especially after my father's passing. They've been my comfort, strength, and inspiration for most of my adult life. And that lifelong inspiration began when I snapped my first photograph as an impressionable twelve-year-old girl."

JACKIE SKAGGS is public affairs officer for Grand Teton National Park and the John D. Rockefeller, Jr. Memorial Parkway, and serves as the official spokesperson on behalf of the park's superintendent. She began her NPS career at Grand Teton in 1984 as a seasonal ranger in visitor services (fee collection); she spent ten years as a seasonal ranger in the Division of Interpretation, seven years as a public affairs specialist, and the past eight years as the public affairs officer. Jackie earned a BA in elementary education from Idaho

DESTINATION

49

State University in Pocatello and completed additional post-graduate classes in the natural sciences.

If You Go

▶ **Getting There:** Several carriers fly into the Jackson Hole airport, including United (800-864-8331; www.united.com) and Frontier Airlines (800-432-1359; www.flyfrontier.com). Many visitors will opt to fly into Salt Lake City, which is a roughly six-hour drive to the park.

▶ **Best Time to Visit:** The campgrounds in Grand Teton National Park are generally open from late May through October. The summer months have the most reliable weather (and crowds); late spring and early fall can be magical.

▶ **Campgrounds:** There are seven campgrounds at GTNP, and they all operate on a first-come, first-served basis. Sites are $22 for tent campers. Reservations (800-628-9988) for group camping are accepted at Colter Bay and Headwaters Campgrounds & RV sites. Full hookups for RVs are available here. Visit www.nps.gov/grte for more details.

▶ **Activities:** Hiking, wildlife viewing, boating, river rafting, horseback riding, rock climbing, and fishing. Ranger-led activities include wildlife walks, hikes, bike tours and campfire programs.

YELLOWSTONE NATIONAL PARK

RECOMMENDED BY **Al Nash**

"I've found that many people have preconceptions about Yellowstone before arriving," began Al Nash. "They've heard of Old Faithful—a place where hot water shoots out of the ground. And they know about the big log lodge—that is, the inn at Old Faithful. They may also know that Yellowstone is a place where you can see bears. I think that the biggest challenge people face is grasping the size of the place. There's a limited amount of the park that you can see on a three-day visit—or even a longer visit. People often ask about the best way to see the park. I don't know if there's a best way. There are two things I do encourage people to do when they're visiting. First, remember that you're on vacation and slow down. You don't travel quickly in Yellowstone—you haven't really experienced the park until you've been in a 'wildlife jam!' [That is, a traffic backup caused by people stopped or pulled over to observe a wild animal along the roadside.] The second piece of advice I offer is to step out of the car and see the park by foot. If you only do a 'windshield tour' you're not getting the full experience. You don't have a sense of being in the wilderness if you're at Old Faithful in the middle of July. But even there, you can find a trailhead and in thirty minutes have a completely different experience. It's easy to get away from the crowds without too much effort.

"Some of my earliest memories as a child involve Yellowstone—the excitement of seeing animals, the smell of the thermal areas, my mom herding my siblings and I back to the car as my dad took a picture of a bear. I equated Yellowstone with awe, wonder, and excitement. Yellowstone can tap those feelings in any individual if they are open to it."

Tucked into the northwest corner of Wyoming and spilling over into parts of Montana and Idaho, Yellowstone is America's and the world's first national park, dedicated in 1872. The first European to spy Yellowstone and its otherworldly geothermal attractions is

believed to be John Colter, who first arrived in current-day Montana as a member of the Corps of Discovery. He parted with Lewis and Clark as the Corps made their way east in the summer of 1806 and began exploring the region that would become known as Yellowstone the following year. His descriptions of the region's geysers and fumaroles were met with derision by many of his contemporaries, who sometimes called the region "Colter's Hell."

Yellowstone encompasses 3,400 square miles of forest, grassland, and wetland terrain, most of which rests at an altitude above 7,700 feet; it's one of the largest intact temperate-zone ecosystems remaining in the world. The park is synonymous with large mammals—bison, elk, moose, pronghorn, bighorn sheep, mule deer, white-tailed deer, black bears—and most famously, grizzly bears and wolves. But it was Yellowstone's unique geothermal properties, not its abundant animal life, that prompted Congress and Ulysses S. Grant to dedicate the park; Yellowstone contains more than 10,000 geysers, hot springs, mudpots, and fumaroles. (Two-thirds of the world's geysers are found here.) There are roughly 300 miles of public roads within the park. The most popular route for visitors is the Grand Loop Road, which makes a 140-mile figure eight through the middle of the park. Many of Yellowstone's iconic landmarks are in proximity to the Grand Loop, including Old Faithful, Yellowstone Lake, Grand Canyon of the Yellowstone, and Mammoth Hot Springs. (Old Faithful geyser erupts roughly every ninety-one minutes, if you were wondering.) A hike that can be accessed along the loop is Mount Washburn, and Al strongly recommends it. "You join the trailhead at Dunraven Pass, and the trail was once a road—though you wouldn't think so, as there are so many switchbacks. It's about three miles one way and fairly strenuous at times, but it's worth it. The views from the fire lookout (at more than ten thousand feet) are nothing short of astounding. On a clear day, you can see forty or fifty miles in every direction."

There are twelve campgrounds in Yellowstone with a total of more than 2,100 sites available. "We have a wide range of front-country opportunities," Al explained. "If you travel in an RV and prefer hookups, the Fishing Bridge RV Park is the only option, but several of the other large campgrounds—Canyon, Grant Village, and Madison—can accommodate anything from small tents to bus-style RVs. These campgrounds [and Bridge Bay] all accept reservations, and they are highly recommended during the high season. These spots all offer the classic national-park large-campground experience. The restrooms have flush toilets and there's potable water. Each also has an amphitheater and

OPPOSITE:
Yellowstone has
more geothermal
activity than
any place else in
the world. It is
also home to a
host of the Rocky
Mountain's most
iconic animals.

DESTINATION

50

a nightly ranger program. Each ranger brings his or her own background and expertise to their program; many have been here twenty or thirty years. If you've never attended one of these programs, you don't know what you're missing. Yellowstone also has seven first-come, first-served campgrounds that offer a smaller campground experience. These campgrounds have water; some have flush toilets, some vault. The first-come, first-served campgrounds fill really early. It breaks my heart to see visitors driving around late in the afternoon, trying to find a spot. They're probably not going to have much luck.

"If you're a first-time visitor to Yellowstone, I'd suggest you make a reservation at one of the larger campgrounds. Once you get the lay of the land, you're better equipped to look at the first-come, first-served sites. If you have to rely on a first-come, first-served site, plan to get to the campground where you want to get a site first thing in the morning."

A chance to view Yellowstone's iconic residents is a big part of the experience for many visitors. While sometimes you'll get lucky and come upon a herd of elk or a bear as you're driving along the Loop Road, it helps to have a plan. "I always encourage visitors to think about the animal you're hoping to see—its habitats and how it lives—when you're looking for it," Al advised. "If you're walking through Mammoth Hot Springs in the middle of August and are disappointed that you haven't seen a bear, consider if you'd want to be around all that thermal activity if you were wearing a fur coat? You'd probably rather be up at a higher elevation and in the shade! Bears—and many other animals—are most active in the cooler parts of the day, and they're going to be where the food is. Part of our goal at the visitor centers is to help people have the best possible experience in the park. Stop and ask rangers where the best places are to look for the animal you're hoping to see. If you have persistence and a bit of luck, you'll be rewarded with an amazing wildlife experience . . . though it's important to remember that all of these animals are truly wild. They can run faster than you and can injure you if they take offense to your presence. I'm wary of all of our wildlife. Visitors should be too."

AL NASH began his National Park Service career as a seasonal ranger-naturalist in Yellowstone in 1995, after a lengthy career in radio and television news. He worked in a variety of positions in interpretation, wildland fire, and public affairs in Yosemite National Park, Indiana Dunes National Lakeshore, and NPS Headquarters in Washington, D.C., before returning to Yellowstone as the park's chief of public affairs in January 2006. Al began his broadcast career in his home state of Michigan, starting as a Top 40 disc jockey at the college radio station while earning a BS in television production at Ferris State University. His television career began at WOI-TV, the ABC affiliate in Des Moines, as he completed an MS in journalism and mass communications at Iowa State University. He first came to the Northern Rockies in 1986 as news director of the Montana Television Network. During his seven years at KTVQ-2 in Billings, he helped guide the CBS network–affiliated stations in establishing award-winning, independent local news operations in Billings, Great Falls, Missoula, and Butte. Al enjoys hiking, camping, backpacking, snowshoeing, and cross-country skiing. An avid private pilot, he is an active volunteer of the Civil Air Patrol, where he holds the rank of lieutenant colonel and serves as both chief of staff of CAP's Montana Wing and director of public affairs for the organization's five-state Rocky Mountain Region.

If You Go

▶ **Getting There:** Visitors can fly into West Yellowstone via Salt Lake City on SkyWest Airlines (www.skywest.com) or Bozeman, Montana roughly two hours from the park's west entrance, which is served by several carriers, including Alaska Airlines (800-252-7522; www.alaskaair.com) and Delta (800-221-1212; www.delta.com).

▶ **Best Time to Visit:** Some campgrounds open as early as May 1, others in mid-June. Most close by early October. July and August have the warmest weather and the biggest crowds. September can be lovely, though there's always a chance of snow.

▶ **Campgrounds:** There are twelve campgrounds in Yellowstone; five (Madison, Fishing Bridge RV Park, Bridge Bay, Canyon, and Grant Village) accept advance reservations (866-439-7375; www.YellowstoneNationalParkLodges.com). The other seven campgrounds (Mammoth, Norris, Tower Fall, Indian Creek, Pebble Creek, Slough Creek, and Lewis Lake) are first come, first served . . . and competition for space during peak season is fierce.

▶ **Activities:** Wildlife viewing, hiking, boating, biking, fishing, and horseback riding.

Published in 2016 by Stewart, Tabori & Chang
An imprint of ABRAMS

Photograph credits: Page 2: Tim Rains, National Park Service; Page 8: Sean Bagshaw; Page 12: Longitude 131°,
Northern Territory, Australia; Page 14: Adirondack Regional Tourism Council; Page 16: Patrick J. Endres/
AlaskaPhotoGraphics.com; Page 22: Kent Miller, National Park Service; Page 26: Parks Canada/Ryan Bray; Page
30: Michael Quinn, National Park Service; Page 36: National Parks Service; Page 38: Parks Australia & Jon Harris
Photography; Page 46: Luke O'Brien Photography; Page 50: Tony Rath Photography/TonyRath.com; Page 54:
Andrew Howard, Wilderness Safaris; Page 58: Parks Canada/J. McCulloch; Page 62: Maria Kraynova/
Shutterstock.com; Page 66: Thomas Zagler/Shutterstock.com; Page 72: Pung/Shutterstock.com; Page 74:
Cascada Expediciones/Torres del Paine National Park, Chile; Page 78: Alexey Stiop/Shutterstock.com; Page 82:
James Cook; Page 88: Deatonphotos/Shutterstock.com; Page 94: Erwin Reiter Photography; Page 98: Adrienne
Baisch/BlackPinePhotography.com; Page 102: Bildagentur Zoonar GmbH/Shutterstock.com; Page 106: National
Park Service; Page 110: Stacy Cramp; Page 114: QT Luong/TerraGallaria.com; Page 120: National Parks Service;
Page 124: Lisa Ridenour Hansen/AllWestYellowstone.com; Page 130: Steve Allen/Shutterstock.com; Page 136:
Greg Stahl; Page 140: Adirondack Regional Tourism Council; Page 144: CreativeNature R.Zwerver/Shutterstock.
com; Page 148: Matthew Williams-Ellis/Robert Harding; Page 154: Parks Canada/J. Pleau; Page 158: Parks
Canada; Page 162: National Park Service; Page 166: Sean Bagshaw; Page 170: Tyler Roemer; Page 178: Höga
Kusten, Norrfällsviken; Page 182: Georges Reif/Camping Arolla; Page 186: Jose Marines/Shutterstock.com;
Page 190: Opel2b/Shutterstock.com; Page 194: Alex Dibrova/Shutterstock.com; Page 200: George H. H. Huey;
Page 206: National Park Service; Page 210: Galyna Andrushko/Shutterstock.com; Page 214: Danielle Lehle;
Page 220: Neal Herbert, National Park Service

Library of Congress Control Number: 2015949306

ISBN: 978-1-4197-1826-7

Editor: Samantha Weiner
Designer: Anna Christian
Production Manager: Kathleen Gaffney

This book was composed in Interstate, Scala, and Village.

Printed and bound in China
10 9 8 7 6 5 4 3 2 1

Stewart, Tabori & Chang books are available at special discounts when purchased in quantity for premiums
and promotions as well as fundraising or educational use. Special editions can also be created to specification.
For details, contact specialsales@abramsbooks.com or the address below.

THE ART OF BOOKS SINCE 1949

115 West 18th Street
New York, NY 10011
www.abramsbooks.com